100 GREATS IPSWICH TOWN FOOTBALL CLUB

Ray Crawford, one of Ipswich Town's legends, unveils the statue of former Ipswich Town and England manager Sir Alf Ramsey, which stands outside the ground at Portman Road. The ceremony took place on 22 August 2000. The sculptor was Sean Hedges Quinn.

100 GREATS

IPSWICH TOWN FOOTBALL CLUB

TONY GARNETT

TEMPUS

Frans Thijssen fails from the penalty spot against Gary Bailey of Manchester United at Portman Road on 1 March 1980. It hardly mattered at the time, as Ipswich won 6-0. Paul Mariner completed a hat-trick, Alan Brazil scored two and the other came from Thijssen. Kevin Beattie also missed from the spot that afternoon, or Ipswich might have had eight. At this time, Ipswich were probably the best club side in the land.

First published 2002
Copyright © Archant (Suffolk), 2002

Tempus Publishing Limited
The Mill, Brimscombe Port,
Stroud, Gloucestershire, GL5 2QG

ISBN 0 7524 2719 9

Typesetting and origination by
Tempus Publishing Limited
Printed in Great Britain by
Midway Colour Print, Wiltshire

Also available by the same author, the *Images of Sport* series book on Ipswich Town contains over 200 illustrations with detailed captions from the history of the club. The book is priced at £10.99.

Tony Garnett.

Introduction

Readers of the *East Anglian Daily Times* recently voted in an 'All-time Top 100 Ipswich Town Football Club Players' Poll'. Players from earlier decades, never seen by many of the voters, inevitably missed out. How else could the most recent David Johnson finish ahead of the first player of that name who played for England and also won honours with Liverpool? Kevin Beattie was the readers' choice as top player. Unfortunately, his career was ended prematurely by injury. Before that, an unfortunate burning accident in 1976 perhaps cost Ipswich Town the Championship. I opted for Paul Mariner, one of the most complete England centre forwards of the century. Strikers tend to capture the headlines, but Mariner was exceptional. It is, however, all a matter of opinion.

Just for interest's sake, the readers' top 100 were as follows:
1-10 Kevin Beattie, John Wark, Arnold Muhren, Mick Mills, Frans Thijssen, Paul Mariner, Terry Butcher, Ray Crawford, Allan Hunter, George Burley.
11-20 Matt Holland, Ted Phillips, Richard Wright, Billy Baxter, Kieron Dyer, Alan Brazil, Paul Cooper, Marcus Stewart, Mick Stockwell, Trevor Whymark.
21-30 Clive Woods, Eric Gates, Mauricio Taricco, Colin Viljoen, John Elsworthy, Russell Osman, Brian Talbot, Jason Dozzell, Titus Bramble, Jimmy Leadbetter.
31-40 James Scowcroft, Alex Mathie, Danny Hegan, Roger Osborne, Tony Mowbray, Martijn Reuser, Jim Magilton, Jimmy Robertson, David Linighan, David Johnson (1990s).
41-50 Chris Kiwomya, Jamie Clapham, Roy Bailey, Hermann Hreidarsson, Simon Milton, Romeo Zondervan, Craig Forrest, Bobby Petta, Tommy Parker, David Johnson (1970s).
51-60 Frank Brogan, Kevin Wilson, Jimmy McLuckie, Andy Nelson, Dalian Atkinson, Bontcho Guentchev, Ian Marshall, Billy Reed, David Geddis, Fabian Wilnis.
61-70 Geraint Williams, Richard Naylor, Steve McCall, Neil Thompson, Gavin Johnson, Mark Venus, Steve Whitton, Tom Garneys, Bryan Hamilton, Danny Sonner.
71-80 Alun Armstrong, Trevor Putney, Peter Morris, Mick Burns, Derek Jefferson, Mich D'Avray, Jason Cundy, Sergei Baltacha, Glenn Pennyfather, Paul Mason.
81-90 Colin Harper, David Best, Dai Rees, Kenny Malcolm, Steve Sedgley, Joe Broadfoot, John McGreal, Frank Yallop, John O'Rourke, Laurie Sivell.
91-100 Gus Uhlenbeek, Jackie Little, David Gregory, Paul Goddard, Ian Cranson, Doug Moran, Mick Lambert, Rod Belfitt, Jermaine Wright, Les Tibbott.

I was once asked what I regretted most about professional football at Portman Road over the past forty-five years. It must be the lack of understanding and communication between the club's two

Bobby Robson, one of the club's most successful managers.

outstanding managers, Sir Alf Ramsey and Sir Bobby Robson. Both worked wonders for the club, both coached England with distinction and both were subsequently honoured with knighthoods. They both have statues around Portman Road – fortunately out of kicking distance of one another.

Ramsey won the World Cup in 1966 but, more importantly, he earned the respect and loyalty of his players. In his autobiography, *An Englishman Abroad*, Robson attacked Alf in apparent retaliation for criticism in a ghosted column in a national newspaper. The Football Association should have looked after Alf far better in retirement. He should never have felt the need to put his name to newspaper articles. There is no doubt about that and Robson knows the score about ghosted articles. Robson purports to be especially upset because he claims that Alf refused to pass on help over conditions in Mexico (Alf was there in 1970 and Bobby in 1986). This was not entirely true. Bobby rang me to ask if I could arrange for him to meet Alf. A meeting was set up, but there was no sign of Bobby – to this day I have had no explanation as to what went wrong. All I know is that a frustrated Ramsey was on the phone to say that Bobby did not appear. Robson wrote: 'The man I could really have had serious help from was Sir Alf, as he had actually experienced the problems we were about to face, but such was our relationship because of his vitriolic attacks in the *Daily Mirror* that it was never possible … I felt totally betrayed by the man who lived just a few streets away from me and who managed Ipswich Town and England so successfully.'

Robson also criticised Bobby Ferguson, his first-team coach and successor as manager at Portman Road. This, I feel, was a sequel to a series of articles written by Bobby Ferguson in the *East Anglian Daily Times*, in which he made valid points about his time as coach under Robson and his period as manager at Portman Road. The decision to increase the capacity of the Pioneer Stand, for which Robson claims to have had the casting vote, became a crippling financial burden. It was a millstone round his successor's neck. Robson knows that football is a team game, both behind the scenes and on the field. One of his strengths has always been to make sound appointments: any glory should be shared.

I have drawn on personal memories, which I hope you will find interesting. Some will show how professional football has changed during the last four-and-a-half decades. There were times when I

The biggest star ever to wear an Ipswich Town shirt was perhaps George Best, who turned out for Bobby Robson's testimonial match in 1979.

would go down to Portman Road and find myself helping to answer the phones when the office staff were hard pressed. I ghosted the programme club notes in the time of Ramsey, Milburn and McGarry. Now, the club has advanced with a superb stadium that is unrecognisable from the homely wooden buildings from which the English champions of 1961/62 emerged.

In the early days, when I first covered Ipswich Town matches, there was no local radio and the national newspapers were not too interested in a club in the Second Division. The reporter covering each club used to be welcomed in opposition boardrooms. I recall a night match against Derby County at the Baseball Ground. By the time I had phoned my report the ground was virtually empty. I heard voices in the boardroom, knocked on the door, and found County manager Harry Storer with a bottle of whisky in one hand and a glass in the other. Ipswich chairman Johnny Cobbold was drinking the whisky as fast as it was being poured. Alf Ramsey, on the other hand, did not want to return to the hotel in any way the worse for wear and was discreetly pouring his whisky into a bowl of flowers. When I arrived I was given a glass that was duly filled. It was most welcome.

I always remember an open fire, scones with strawberry jam and cream and home-made cakes in the oak-panelled Blackburn Rovers Board Room at Ewood Park before the ground was redeveloped. They were good old days.

I am grateful to those who worked so meticulously to produce the statistics. Books such as *The Men Who Made The Town* by John Eastwood and Tony Moyes were invaluable. So was the encyclopaedic *Ipswich Town, The Modern Era* by Robert Hadgraft. I also read Bobby Robson's books, *Time On The Grass* and *An Englishman Abroad, My Autobiography*. Sharon Boswell hunted out the pictures that I needed. I am also grateful to the *East Anglian Daily Times* photographers over the decades, whose work I have been able to plunder.

In the statistics supplied for the players I have chosen for this book, the Ipswich career records refer to the Football League Cup, regardless of the particular sponsors. The same ruling applies to the short-lived Full Members' Cup.

Tony Garnett,
July 2002

100 Ipswich Town Greats

Ian Atkins
Dalian Atkinson
Roy Bailey
Gerry Baker
Sergei Baltacha
Bill Baxter
Kevin Beattie
Rod Belfitt
David Best
Titus Bramble
Alan Brazil
Mark Brennan
Joe Broadfoot
Frank Brogan
George Burley
Terry Butcher
Larry Carberry
Tommy Carroll
Frank Clarke
John Colrain
John Compton
Paul Cooper
Ian Cranson
Ray Crawford
Jason Cundy
Mich D'Avray
Jason Dozzell
Kieron Dyer
John Elsworthy
Craig Forrest
Tom Garneys
Eric Gates
Brian Gayle
David Geddis

Nigel Gleghorn
Paul Goddard
Bontcho Guentchev
Bryan Hamilton
Ken Hancock
Colin Harper
Danny Hegan
Mick Hill
Matt Holland
Tony Humes
Allan Hunter
Derek Jefferson
David Johnson (Jonty)
David Johnson
Chris Kiwomya
Mick Lambert
Cyril Lea
Jimmy Leadbetter
David Linighan
David Lowe
Steve McCall
Jimmy McLuckie
Mick McNeil
Ken Malcolm
Paul Mariner
Ian Marshall
Paul Mason
Alex Mathie
Mick Mills
Doug Millward
Simon Milton
Doug Moran
Peter Morris
Tony Mowbray

Arnold Muhren
Andy Nelson
Roger Osborne
Russell Osman
Tommy Parker
Bobby Petta
Ted Phillips
Reg Pickett
Trevor Putney
Billy Reed
Doug Rees
Jimmy Robertson
James Scowcroft
Steve Sedgley
Laurie Sivell
Roy Stephenson
Mick Stockwell
Alan Sunderland
Brian Talbot
Mauricio Taricco
Frans Thijssen
Claus Thomsen
Neil Thompson
Colin Viljoen
John Wark
Trevor Whymark
Geraint Williams
Kevin Wilson
Clive Woods
Richard Wright
Frank Yallop
Romeo Zondervan

Although a few players have two pages instead of one, this in no way indicates any order of merit. It is purely to tell the story of their time in greater detail or to use pictures of special interest. My top twenty, though, are in italics.

Ian Atkins

Defender, 1985 to 1988

Born: Birmingham, 16 January 1957
Signed: September 1985 from Everton for
    £100,000
Debut: *v.* Leicester City (away), lost 0-1,
    28 September 1985

Ipswich career:
94 starts (4 subs), 4 goals
Football League 73(4), 4
Play-offs: 2
FA Cup: 4
Football League Cup: 8
Full Members' Cup: 7

Other clubs (as player, coach or manager): Shrewsbury
    Town, Sunderland, Everton, Birmingham City,
    Colchester United, Doncaster Rovers,
    Northampton Town and Oxford United.

Ian Atkins arrived at Portman Road as a commanding personality and a veteran captain, lending considerable experience to a young team. Even so, he was unable to prevent Town from dropping out of the First Division for the first time in eighteen years in 1986. Losing the stalwart Terry Butcher for so long with a knee injury added enormously to the task of staying up. The fact that Ipswich fans at the time were disenchanted and seemed unable to comprehend the problems of having to sell star players to fund the extension to the Pioneer Stand did not help either. The following season, Ipswich had massive injury problems when they lost to Charlton in the play-off semi-final over two legs. Manager Bobby Ferguson departed. He went on to take up a position with Al Arabi in Kuwait, where his coaching ability bore fruit and was rewarded with a cup and league double.

Ferguson sensed that his time was up at Portman Road. After the second leg defeat at Selhurst Park, he travelled back to Ipswich in my car rather than travel on the team bus. Parting with Ferguson was a mistake by the Ipswich directors. Promotion the following season would have been likely, but pressure from the fans – particularly some of the box-holders – played a part in bringing an end to his reign. In the meantime, Atkins did not see eye to eye with new boss John Duncan. He returned from injury to play in the starting line-up at Millwall on 12 September. Atkins, as club captain, expected to lead the team out but was told at the last moment, while in the toilet, that he had been deposed. His deputy, Ian Cranson, retained the armband. This just about ended the relationship. The following March, Atkins moved to Birmingham City for £30,000 while Cranson, quite a star in the Town squad, was sold to Sheffield Wednesday.

The following summer Ipswich paid Shrewsbury Town £300,000 for David Linighan to bolster the defence. Atkins had started at Shrewsbury but followed manager Alan Durban to Sunderland in April 1982.

Atkins was with Colchester United in their first season in the Conference. Since then he has had spells with Doncaster Rovers, Carlisle United, Cambridge United, Northampton Town and Oxford United.

9

Born: Shrewsbury, 21 March 1968
Signed: 4 June 1985 from apprentice
Debut: *v.* Newcastle United (away), lost 1-3,
    15 March 1986

Ipswich career:
59 starts (13 subs), 22 goals
Football League: 49(11), 18
Play-offs: 2
FA Cup: 1
Football League Cup: 5(1), 3
Full Members' Cup: 2(1), 1
Honours: England B caps

Other clubs: Sheffield Wednesday, Real
    Sociedad, Aston Villa, Fenerbahce and
    Manchester City (loan).

Dalian Atkinson had exciting pace and a terrific finish. Town supporters will always remember his thrilling hat-trick against a Middlesborough defence that included Tony Mowbray and Gary Pallister in April 1988. Atkinson was top marksman with 13 goals the following season, but he was not particularly easy for a manager to handle and John Duncan sold him to Ron Atkinson's Sheffield Wednesday for a paltry £450,000 in July 1989. This was made to look like chickenfeed when Atkinson, after winning England B honours, moved to Real Sociedad for £1.7 million in August 1990. It was galling that Ipswich had no sell-on clause; Dalian's quality had always been obvious.

In July 1991, Dalian rejoined Ron Atkinson, now at Aston Villa – it was there that a journal-ist asked Big Ron how 'his son' was getting on! Dalian missed an Ipswich visit to Villa Park and Ron explained : 'He had a fitness test. I threw a ball at him and he said "ouch" before it reached him'. Dalian scored in Villa's 3-1 Coca-Cola Cup victory over Manchester United in 1994. His next stop was a spell with Fenerbahce in Turkey, whom he joined for £600,000 in July 1995.

On his return to England, he went on loan to Manchester City and reappeared at Portman Road in April 1997, looking more like Frank Bruno than his old self. He headed against the bar, but Ipswich won with a first-half penalty, converted by Steve Sedgley.

My lasting memory of Dalian was when I agreed, foolishly, to drive his Alfa Romeo to Sheffield one Friday afternoon, so that he could use the car after the match at Bramall Lane. The car looked like a stick of pink-and-0white pep-permint rock. It stalled when going slowly. Neither the foot or handbrake worked.

When I started flicking switches to try and find the lights, all I succeeded in doing was changing the music. Suffice to say, I was unable to hold the car on one of the many Sheffield hills in the rush hour. The car stalled, and then rolled back, breaking the light of the vehicle behind. I paid for the damage, but Dalian was never convinced that the incident ever happened! I have been wary of driving footballers' cars ever since.

Roy Bailey

Goalkeeper, 1956 to 1965

Born: Epsom 26 May 1932
Died: April 1993
Signed: 15 March 1956 from Crystal Palace
Debut: *v.* Norwich City (away), lost 2-3,
      2 April 1956

Ipswich career:
348 starts, no goals
Football League: 315
FA Cup: 19
Football League Cup: 7
European Cup: 4
FA Charity Shield: 1
Other matches: 2

Other club: Crystal Palace

Roy was born in Epsom on Derby Day in 1932, the fifth child of thirteen (April The Fifth was the Derby winner). During the war he was evacuated to Somerset, where he went to school in Weston-super-Mare. He was fifteen when he returned to Surrey where he, and his brother David, played for Tottenham Juniors. Travelling from Epsom to North London became a hassle for the lads, so they joined nearby Crystal Palace as amateurs. Roy was employed by his uncle as a painter and decorator before National Service in Germany, where he played for the British Army on the Rhine. He made his League debut for Palace in a 3-1 defeat at Torquay when he was seventeen years old, but did not play regular League football until his Army service was completed. He played 118 League games for Palace before Alf Ramsey signed him just prior to the transfer deadline in March 1956.

His Ipswich debut, against Norwich City at Carrow Road, had a nightmare start, as he had to pick the ball out of the back of the net twice in the opening three minutes. It was not long, though, before he displaced George McMillan as Town's regular first choice. His form during Ipswich Town's glory years of 1960 to 1962 was spectacular, but things started to go wrong as the defence in front of him began to fall apart. He won Third Division (South), Second Division and First Division championship medals and held an FA coaching badge. He was also an MCC-qualified cricket coach and kept wicket for the club side, Ipswich & East Suffolk.

I recall playing against Ipswich & East Suffolk at Chantry Park for Saxmundham. Roy was keeping wicket when he sent a message asking me to push his son's pram round the boundary until the lad fell asleep. The baby in question was Gary, who went on to play for Manchester United and won 2 caps for England in 1985. Roy emigrated to South Africa, where he became national coach and, later, took up media work with such success that he became as well known in his adopted country as Jimmy Hill became in England.

Gary is carrying on in the same tradition as his late father. During the Championship-winning season of 1961/62, Bailey bet me that I could not beat him with three successive penalty kicks. The opportunity did not arise until the end-of-season tour on the ground of Holstein Kiel. I was fired up and scored all three times. Then reserve goalkeeper, Wilf Hall, wanted the same bet. I stupidly took him on and put my first shot high over the bar. Football takes itself far too seriously for anything like that to happen these days.

Gerry Baker was the brother of Joe Baker, who won 8 caps for England while with Hibernian and Arsenal. Gerry cost £17,000 from Hibernian and came to Portman Road with one amazing record to his name: he scored ten goals for St Mirren in their 15-0 Scottish Cup demolition of Glasgow University. Later, his brother Joe scored nine in a cup tie against Peebles Rovers and missed a penalty in a 15-1 win.

Baker scored in the six successive matches that followed the 0-0 draw on his debut, but he could not save Ipswich from relegation. In the third round of the FA Cup he completed his hat-trick at home to Oldham in 19 minutes; Ipswich led 5-1 after 43 minutes and won 6-3. The fourth round at home to Stoke City was memorable, but not for Baker who was off injured from the ninth minute. It was the only time the great Stanley Matthews set foot on Portman Road, and he was just short of his forty-ninth birthday. Ipswich drew 1-1, but lost the replay at the Victoria Ground to a mishit shot from Jimmy McIlroy. I remember criticising the team for their negative approach to a cup tie after falling behind. About seven weeks later, Ipswich returned to Stoke City for the League match and crashed 9-1 – having had equal possession only to be caught on the break time after time.

Gerry had a tale about manager Bill McGarry, who once said: 'There are sixteen Scotsmen here and they'll all be gone at the end of the season.' Gerry piped up in a broad

Born: New York, 11 April 1938
Signed: 5 December 1963 from Hibernian for £17,000
Debut: v. Blackburn Rovers (home), 0-0, 7 December 1963

Ipswich career:
151 starts, 66 goals
Football League: 135, 58
FA Cup: 9, 4
Football League Cup: 7, 4
Honours: 4 caps for United States

Other clubs: Chelsea, St Mirren, Manchester City, Hibernian, Coventry City and Brentford.

Scottish accent: 'But I'm an American.' Bill was less than amused.

The Baker family lived not far from the Belstead Arms public house on the Chantry Estate. His daughters, Karen and Lorraine, both represented Great Britain at athletics. Karen was a 400-metre runner, while Lorraine finished fifth in the 800 metres in the Los Angeles Olympics. Gerry joined Coventry City for £20,000 in November 1967. At the end of his career he was player-manager of Margate and also played for Nuneaton Borough, as well as other non-League sides. He worked as an auto-electrician for Jaguar in Coventry, but more recently has taken up landscape gardening.

Gerry Baker (extreme left) shakes hands with manager Jackie Milburn, watched by (from left) John Compton, Dennis Thrower and Danny Hegan.

Sergei Baltacha
Sweeper, 1989 to 1990

Born: Ukraine, 17 February 1958
Signed: January 1989 from Dynamo Kiev
Debut: *v.* Stoke City (home), won 5-1,
    21 January 1989

Ipswich career:
24 starts (6 sub), 1 goal
Football League: 22 (6), 1
Football League Cup: 1
Full Members' Cup: 1
Honours: 46 Soviet Union international caps

Other clubs: Metallist Kharkov, Dynamo Kiev,
    St Johnstone and Inverness Caledonian Thistle.

The first-ever Soviet player to appear in the Football League was very popular with Town fans, yet they never really had the opportunity to see him do the job at which he was a specialist.

He had been an immaculate sweeper for the USSR for a long time before Ipswich manager John Duncan took the adventurous step of bringing him to England from Dynamo Kiev. Baltacha did not speak English at first, so it was considered a risk to put him in the defence until he had settled down.

Instead, he made his debut on the right of midfield in a home match with Stoke City. He brought the house down when he opened the scoring early in the second half with a tap-in. Ipswich went on to win 5-1. Of course he was out of position, but that did not stop him from making the most of a cross from Chris Kiwomya. Why Duncan never established his popular new star as a sweeper, which would have meant a radical change of club tactics, remains a mystery. He must have known that Baltacha was a sweeper in the style of Bobby Moore, rather than an orthodox central defender, when he made the signing.

David Sheepshanks, then a young director, went to the Ukraine with Duncan to assist in the negotiations with the Soviets. Sergei duly arrived with his wife Olga, a former international pentathlete, son Sergei and daughter Elena. The lad, a big hit in youth football down Whitton way, grew up to play for St Mirren and win under-21 honours for Scotland. Elena became an excellent tennis player who hit the headlines at Wimbledon 2002. The Baltacha family lived in a rented house off Hadleigh Road in Ipswich. Their neighbour, Bob Shelley, helped the family to settle in a new country.

Part of the Baltacha deal was that Ipswich Town should visit the Ukraine in the next pre-season. The Town chairman at the time was Patrick Cobbold, who thoroughly enjoyed the succession of obligatory toasts in vodka. When meeting one top Soviet commissar (the Iron Curtain was still up) Patrick broke the ice by announcing: 'Do you know, Harold Macmillan is my uncle?' This broke the ice and led to back-slapping, laughter and, of course, vodka. David Sheepshanks broke his arm falling into an unlit deep pothole at an airport during this trip.

Baltacha was never strong in the air, so struggled as a member of an orthodox back four. Ipswich coach Charlie Woods would certainly not have recommended him to Duncan's successor, John Lyall. Perhaps Woods felt that recruiting Baltacha was a gimmick. After all, Duncan had hit the headlines previously when he selected cricketer Ian Botham to play for Scunthorpe United. On a similar theme, Alf Ramsey once invited singer Tommy Steele to play for Ipswich reserves after seeing him in a showbiz team – that offer was declined.

I take the view that Baltacha could have been a class sweeper for Ipswich, if only he had been given the opportunity.

Bill Baxter

Wing half and central defender, 1960 to 1971

Born: Edinburgh, 23 April 1939
Signed: 10 June 1960 from Broxburn Athletic
Debut: v. Norwich City (home), won 4-1,
    27 December 1960

Ipswich career:
459 starts, 22 goals
Football League: 409, 21
FA Cup: 23, 1
Football League Cup: 22
European Cup: 4
FA Charity Shield: 1
Honours: British Army (Kentish Cup)

Other clubs: Hull City, Watford, Northampton
Town (player-manager), Nuneaton Borough
    and Dunfermline.

Bill Baxter was a tough Scot who had been spotted playing for Broxburn Athletic by Ipswich Town scout John Forsyth (brother of Town trainer Jimmy). He arrived at Portman Road in June 1960 but, with the season just starting, he was called up for National Service (in just about the final batch). Baxter was with the Royal Engineers stationed at Farnborough and was soon part of the British Army football team.

His first game for Ipswich was at left-back, when he deputised for fellow Scot, Ken Malcolm, in a 4-1 win over Norwich City on 27 December. He obviously impressed Alf Ramsey, because the following game he was chosen at right half in place of Reg Pickett, who had a stomach muscle strain. Baxter did not miss another match all season as Ipswich carried off the Second Division championship. In only his third appearance, I recall a spectacular goal-line clearance against Liverpool at Anfield at the opposite end to The Kop, which helped Ipswich to a precious 1-1 draw.

After one particularly good display from Baxter that season – and there were many –

I ventured to suggest to Alf Ramsey that I thought the young Scot had done well. 'You would think so', was Alf's reply in a tone of voice that put a young reporter firmly in his place for voicing an opinion.

I once drove to Aldershot on a Friday to bring Baxter to Suffolk for a home match, but it was not too long before he could buy a small Standard car to make the trip by road.

Baxter always seemed to be in the shadow of Frank McLintock for Scottish international honours, although everyone in East Anglia soon became convinced that he was the better player and that it was only because McLintock was with more fashionable clubs (Leicester City and Arsenal) that he was selected.

Baxter helped Ipswich Town to become the first club to win the First Division Championship at the first attempt (other than Preston North End of course, who were the inaugural champions in the 1888/89 season). Ramsey took over England and Jackie Milburn became the new Ipswich Town manager. He inherited an ageing team other than Baxter, who became the star player at Portman Road over the next decade.

There was little one man could do to check the slide. He took over the captaincy from Andy Nelson for the home match with Stoke City on 9 November 1963 and retained the post until the club opted for the extra expe-

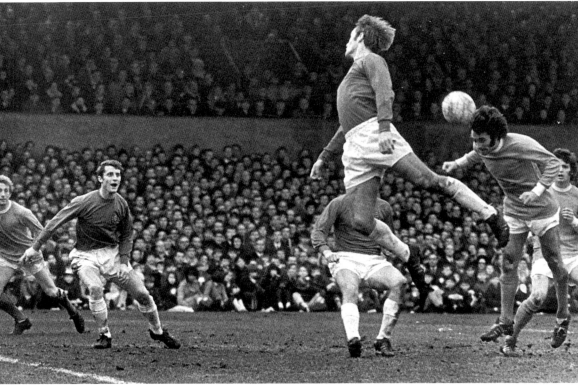

Bill Baxter (second from left), with his eye on the ball, is well aware of famous Scottish international Denis Law in the background as George Best gets his head to the ball despite a leap from Mick Mills in a match against Manchester Utd.

rience of Mick McNeil and then Cyril Lea.

Milburn resigned with Ipswich struggling in the Second Division, shortly preceding a lively shareholders' annual meeting at which Tulip Rally driver Ken Brightwell was elected to the Board as the supporters' choice.

Bill McGarry arrived in October 1964 to crack the whip and rule by a certain amount of fear. It was McGarry who had the vision to switch Baxter to central defence. Even though the Scot stood only 5ft 8in tall, he was a power in the air and seldom lost a header.

Baxter was restored as captain in the 1967/68 season, when Ipswich became Second Division Champions once again. Having guided the club to promotion, McGarry stayed until November the following season, when he decided that the grass was greener in Wolverhampton.

Bobby Robson arrived with Baxter staying in as captain of a club fighting tooth and nail

to stay at the top level. There was soon a personality clash between Baxter and Robson. Apparently, Baxter refused to carry out an order in training and Robson dropped him for the next match at West Ham.

The feud came to boiling point in February 1967 (see the Tommy Carroll story for the details) and sadly Baxter never played for the club again. He was sold to Hull City for £12,000 and did not return to Portman Road until May 2002 for the reunion of Ramsey's 1961/62 Championship-winning side. A more mellow Baxter was willing to forgive and forget; he is, however, still adamant that he was in the right.

His leg has been amputated because of poor circulation as a result of diabetes, but he still plays golf at Dunfermline. He has retired from a job as an engineer with British Telecom.

Kevin Beattie

Defender, 1976 to 1982

Born: Carlisle, 18 December 1953
Signed: 29 July 1971 from youth scheme
Debut: *v.* Manchester United (away), won 2-1,
    12 August 1972

Ipswich career:
297 starts (11 subs), 32 goals
Football League: 225(3), 24 goals
FA Cup: 25(2), 5
Football League Cup: 16, 1
UEFA Cup: 20(6), 2
European Cup Winners' Cup: 3
Texaco Cup: 8
Honours: 9 full England caps, 9 under-23 caps and
    England youth caps

Other clubs: Colchester United, Carlisle United
    and Middlesbrough.

Kevin Beattie was an outstanding footballer, compared by many to the late Duncan Edwards (the legendary Manchester United half-back, who was killed in the Munich air disaster). Kevin's power and pace were phenomenal. He could leap higher than his rivals and strike the ball with a venom that was awesome to watch. He could be a match-winner both in domestic football and in Europe. He showed no fear.

Once he broke onto the scene, the honours followed thick and fast. He was PFA Young Player of the Year, the trophy being handed over by Don Revie. He was Rothmans Youth Player of the Year, with Sir Alf Ramsey making the presentation. He was the Ipswich Town supporters' Player of the Year in 1972/73, and in the following season as well.

Beattie always seemed to be in the headlines, but not always for the right reasons. When he was meant to be reporting to the England under-23 squad at Aberdeen he felt a bit homesick and took the train to Carlisle instead to visit his parents. He was tracked down having a pint and playing dominoes in the Magpie pub near his home. He was fortunate to escape unscathed when his Opel car overturned near Shotley, where the Town squad had been training. Kevin, John Wark, Dale Roberts and Glen

Westley all managed to climb out of a window unhurt, with the car a mangled write-off.

Then there was the time in the spring of 1977 season, when Kevin suffered severe burns to his face and neck in an accident at his home that remains something of a mystery to this day. The club were considering putting out a statement to the effect that Beattie had thrown paraffin on a bonfire which had exploded back at him; paraffin was changed to petrol on my recommendation, as it seemed more believable. Whatever the cause, this accident probably cost Ipswich the League Championship.

On 18 January 1975, Ipswich visited Carlisle who had risen to the First Division. Ipswich lost 2-1, but all I can recall is one of Beattie's sisters – they were a large family – taking a shine to Trevor Whymark and having to be physically ejected from the team coach before it could start its journey south. Beattie was so valuable to the Ipswich team that it was always a massive blow when he was missing. He broke his arm in the FA Cup semi-final defeat against Manchester City at Villa Park in 1981, which turned out to be his farewell appearance.

The worst of his injury problems started in October 1977, when he hurt his knee with the England squad in Luxembourg. He underwent a cartilage operation and returned to play a reserve match twenty-five days later. The following month he was in the Ipswich team that beat Barcelona 3-0 at Portman Road. Medical opinion remains divided as to whether he came back too soon. This was before the days of key-hole surgery but the lad was desperate to play. Beattie was a colossus – there is no question about that.

He had a spell in Scandinavia, but since his playing days ended he has had problems with his health and underwent an emergency stomach operation in Ipswich in March 1991. He has taken up media work.

The power of Kevin Beattie is apparent both in the air and on the ground. Right: He gets in a shot against Manchester United goalkeeper Alex Stepney despite a challenge from George Graham. Below: He rises to head powerfully away from the challenge of Southampton's Mick Channon at Portman Road with Allan Hunter (no. 5) watching approvingly. Ipswich won that match 7-0. Peter Morris is the Ipswich player on the left of the picture.

Born: Doncaster, 30 October 1945
Signed: 3 November 1971 from Leeds United
for £50,000
Debut: *v.* Wolverhampton Wanderers (home),
won 2-1, 6 November 1971

Ipswich career:
46 starts, 16 goals
Football League: 40, 13
FA Cup: 2
Football League Cup: 1
Texaco Cup: 3, 3

Other clubs: Leeds United, Everton, Sunderland,
Fulham (loan), Huddersfield Town, Worksop
Town. Frickley Athletic and Bentley Victoria.

A useful old-fashioned striker, Belfitt was signed from Leeds United for £50,000 He moved on to Everton as a key member of the deal that brought David Johnson to Portman Road in 1972. The Town fans took to him after he scored on his debut. They were sorry to see him go.

Belfitt was indirectly responsible for giving me my first ever taste of the sort of underhand journalism that convinced me to reject various job opportunities in London. One of the national Sunday tabloids was sniffing after some sort of scandal that involved Don Revie's Leeds United side while Belfitt was at Elland Road. They sent a reporter, with a tape recorder in a slightly open briefcase. They hoped that one of the Ipswich players might have heard something from Belfitt and would let it slip in casual conversation.

I was asked to introduce the reporter to the players in their homes. I felt it best that I knew what was happening rather than be on the outside. I handpicked the players I knew best, warned them what was happening, and saw at first hand how such stories could come about. Bobby Robson was also fully aware of what was happening. Needless to say, no one said anything that could be used out of context to incriminate Leeds in any way. In fact, I very much doubt if there was any justification for the investigation at all. One player kept his television on low while the interview was taking place, which rendered the recording useless.

Rod worked as a draughtsman for a while but then became a financial planning consultant for Allied Dunbar in Doncaster. How many of today's footballers of Belfitt's standard will need to find alternative work when they hang up their boots?

Born: Wareham 6 September 1943

Signed: 16 October 1968 from Oldham Athletic for £25,000

Debut: *v.* Nottingham Forest (on neutral Notts County ground), won 2-1, 19 October 1968

Ipswich career:
199 starts
Football League: 168
FA Cup: 9
Football League Cup: 10
Texaco Cup: 7
UEFA Cup: 5

Other clubs: Bournemouth, Oldham Athletic and Portsmouth. He later managed Dorchester Town and Poole Town amongst others.

David Best was always cool, calm and calculated. When he chased referee Roy Capey to the halfway line at Stamford Bridge, it was evident that something had gone terribly wrong. It was on 26 September 1970 that Alan Hudson's shot from the inside-left channel had hit the stanchion holding up the netting and rebounded back into play. Mr Capey awarded a goal. He was persuaded to consult his linesman by the weight of Ipswich protests, but the goal stood. Chelsea won 2-1 and Ipswich asked the League if the match could be replayed. Of course there was never a chance of that happening, despite the clear injustice. The next match, Best twisted his ankle in a collision with Jeff Astle of West Bromwich. In came little Laurie Sivell who held

his place until the following April, when he broke his finger against Everton.

Best was signed from Oldham by Bill McGarry. They had been together at Bournemouth. On 22 November 1969, Ipswich were playing Stoke City at the Victoria Ground. The previous night Best felt unwell and there was no goalkeeping cover in the travelling squad.

Bobby Robson rang me to check whether I was driving to the match on Saturday morning and, if so, to find Alec Bugg and bring him. The problem was firstly to identify Bugg's boots. I assumed they would be the largest in the boot-room and was proved right. Then came the problem of making contact. As he had no match that weekend and it was a Friday evening he was not expected back at his home at Needham Market until late. I asked his mother to put a note on his pillow that I would be picking him up at 6.30 the following morning and to tell him that he might be required to play.

The roads were slow when towns like Bury St Edmunds, Newmarket, Cambridge and Huntingdon had yet to be by-passed. Sure enough, a bleary-eyed Bugg was ready in time and slept in the car for most of the trip. It was no false alarm. Bugg played what proved to be his fourth and final First Division match in a 3-3 draw. He then moved to Bournemouth, but soon changed his career path and became a policeman. Best was a reliable 'keeper for Ipswich, perhaps behind Richard Wright, Paul Cooper, Roy Bailey and Mick Burns, but on a par with Ken Hancock, Laurie Sivell and Jack Parry.

David Best clears from Joe Royle in a match against Everton at Goodison Park. Howard Kendall (left) is the other Everton player in the picture, together with Ipswich central defenders Bill Baxter and Derek Jefferson.

Defender, 1998 to 2002

Born: Ipswich, 21 July 1981
Signed: 1 August 1997
Debut: *v.* Sheffield United (away), won 2-1,
    20 December 1998

Ipswich career:
53 starts (9 subs), 1 goal
Football League: 2(2)
FA Cup: 4(1)
Football League Cup: 4(1), 2
UEFA Cup: 4, 1
Honours: 8 England under-21 caps

Other clubs: Colchester United (loan) and
    Newcastle United.

Ipswich Town's Academy, one of the best in the land, has provided talent that has kept the club afloat financially. Lads like Jason Dozzell, Chris Kiwomya, Kieron Dyer, Richard Wright and Titus Bramble have all moved for big money. Bramble, a pupil at Holywells High School in Ipswich, signed schoolboy forms at Portman Road when he was fourteen. He, and his brother Tesfaye, were dominant figures in junior football in the region. One season he scored 75 goals in a season for Kesgrave Kestrels. He was playing in midfield. An early disappointment was being picked for the England under-16 squad, but having to withdraw because of injury.

He did not have to wait long to emerge as a real talent. He was thrown in at the deep end for his debut against Sheffield United at Bramall Lane in December 1998. He was only seventeen, but had Tony Mowbray alongside to guide him through a 2-1 victory that was shown live on television. The following month he was back in the side against Sunderland in the daunting atmosphere of the Stadium of Light. It was the day Jim Magilton made his Ipswich debut. Although Ipswich lost 2-1, young Bramble enhanced his ever-growing reputation.

He had to battle through a succession of injuries. He broke his leg as a youth player. Then he suffered from tendinitis, the result of rapid growth. The problem was called Osgood's

Sclatter – which is similar to shin splints but with the knee being affected. An ankle injury laid him low for a while. When he was fit again he went on loan to Colchester United but suffered more damage to his leg in a tackle against Bristol Rovers that conceded a penalty and virtually ended his season.

Once Ipswich found themselves in the Premiership, it was thought that Bramble would grow from strength to strength. He burst through on a solo run to score the winner against Sunderland at Portman Road. The power of some of his tackling can be awesome. I watched a reserve match at Norwich when he tackled a slightly-built lad called Pape Diop. It was perfectly fair, but Diop stayed on the ground for a very long time!

One of his heroes was Sol Campbell, with whom he was delighted to swap shirts when they played against each other at Tottenham. He broke into the England under-21 squad and he has been freely tipped for full England honours by Town boss George Burley.

In Ipswich's relegation season of 2001/02, Bramble was suffering from a bone growth on his heel that was making his Achilles tendon sore. Minor surgery was needed to put things right. In the meantime, he was making costly errors and, instead of taking command at the heart of the defence, he found himself below comparative old stagers John McGreal and Mark Venus in the pecking order at Portman Road. He also dropped out of the England under-21 squad.

Born: Glasgow 15 June 1959
Signed: 30 May 1977, from youth scheme
Debut: *v.* Manchester United (home), lost 1-2,
    14 January 1978

Ipswich career:
195 starts (15 subs), 80 goals
Football League: 143(11), 70
FA Cup: 18(2), 6
Football League Cup: 14(1), 3
UEFA Cup: 18(1), 1
European Cup Winners' Cup: 2
Honours: 13 full caps for Scotland (all won at
    Ipswich), 8 under-21 caps and Scottish youth

Other clubs: Tottenham Hotspur, Manchester
    United, Coventry City and QPR.

Alan Brazil, nicknamed Pele for obvious reasons, was as clinical a finisher as any when one-on-one with a goalkeeper. His ammunition in his most prolific seasons at Portman Road was supplied in the main by Arnold Muhren, and he developed a near telepathic understanding with the Dutchman. That's what made it so surprising that, when both joined Manchester United, they were selected together so seldom.

Brazil never enjoyed the sort of success at his other clubs that he did at Ipswich. He became renowned for his terrific interest in horseracing and was often seen at Newmarket and Yarmouth. Knowing how he recognised a good value wager, I once suggested to him that his application to become manager of Ipswich Town in 1994 was not worth the postage stamp needed to apply. He was less than amused, but the indisputable fact was that he stood no chance at that time.

He ran the Black Adder pub in Ipswich for a while, but then took to media work like a duck to water and has made quite a name for himself on Talk Radio. He became part of a syndicate involved with a smart two-year-old called Indian Haven trained by Paul D'Arcy at Newmarket. The colt won on his debut at Yarmouth but Alan, when going to collect his winnings, found that he had mistakenly accepted a ticket for the beaten odds-on favourite. A compromise was reached, but it all goes to show that it pays to check your bets very carefully indeed.

I remember giving Brazil, then a radio pundit, a lift to a match at Coventry where he had been a player. He assured me that he knew a short-cut to the Highfield Road ground. He directed me to Willenhall Greyhound Racing Stadium instead. Maybe I shouldn't have been surprised.

Brazil was in the Ipswich side which won the UEFA Cup in 1981. His only goal in that glorious run came in the 5-0 victory over Widzew Lodz. John Wark, with brilliantly timed runs from the midfield, was the main marksman with 14 goals, while Paul Mariner contributed 6.

Mark Brennan
Midfield, 1983 to 1988

Born: Rossendale 4 October 1965
Signed: 1 April 1983 from youth scheme
Debut: *v.* QPR, FA Cup third round (home), won
3-2, 9 November 1983

Ipswich career:
208 starts (4 subs), 25 goals
Football League: 165(3), 19
Play-offs: 2
FA Cup: 12, 3
Football League Cup: 21(1), 2
Full Members' Cup: 8, 1
Honours: 5 England under-21 caps and youth
international

Other clubs: Middlesbrough, Manchester City,
Oldham Athletic, Sydney Olympic and
Dagenham & Redbridge.

A talented youngster introduced by Town manager Bobby Ferguson, Brennan had a sweet left foot. He dominated the central midfield against Manchester United at Old Trafford in May 1984 against Bryan Robson, when Ipswich ensured First Division survival with a 2-1 victory. Great things were expected, but his international hopes virtually ended when he was one of the 'Toulon Four' who broke a curfew imposed by coach Dave Sexton. He found himself in trouble with the Football Association as a result.

The long-ball game introduced by manager John Duncan did not suit Brennan's style of play. He became disillusioned and not even a heart-to-heart with Duncan, while drinking his favourite 'white top' lager in the manager's office, could convince him to stay at Portman Road (Duncan had asked me what Brennan's favourite drink was so that he could have it ready).

I was playing golf with Brennan at Felixstowe Ferry on the day that his agent, Eric Hall, negotiated his move to Middlesbrough. He had also been in discussions with Robert Chase, the Norwich City chairman. One of Brennan's most embarrassing moments at Ipswich, where he occasionally wore the captain's armband, was when he sliced a penalty kick well wide in a

2-0 home defeat against Derby County in April 1987. It was a terrible miss which he attributed to slipping on the muddy run-up.

There were times when Brennan was without a driving licence. One Sunday around 11 p.m. he rang me and asked if I would do him a favour. He was still in the middle of a frame of snooker with golf professional Tim Spurgeon at Westerfield. He had to report for training with Middlesbrough the next morning, or else he would have been in serious trouble with manager Bruce Rioch – a strong disciplinarian. All the trains had already gone. The question was whether I would be able to drive him back to Middlesbrough to save his bacon. The trip up the A1 did not take too long at dead of night. It was not until he was in the car the next morning to be delivered to the training ground that he pointed out that he needed a lift to Sunderland and not Ayresome Park as I had imagined.

Brennan played for Middlesbrough at the same time as Tony Mowbray. They had houses on opposite sides of the road at the village of Yarm. Then he moved to Manchester City for £400,000 before a spell at Oldham Athletic. He dropped out of the League and played in Sydney and then on the mainland of China. On his return to England he played for Dagenham & Redbridge and worked in a sports hall in that area.

Born: Lewisham, 4 March 1940
Signed: (first time) 16 October 1963 from Millwall
Debut: *v.* Blackpool (away) drew 2-2,
    19 October 1963

Ipswich career:
113 starts (2 sub), 21 goals
Football League: 100(1), 19
FA Cup: 8, 1
Football League Cup: 5(1), 1

Other clubs: Millwall (twice) and Northampton.

Joe Broadfoot was quite a character. On the field he had terrific pace and a thunderbolt shot. He looked knock-kneed but he took some stopping when in full flight and was exciting to watch.

He was also a talented club cricketer with the Old Roan CC in Kent, although he played for Saxmundham while in East Anglia (he once took a spectacular running catch on the extra cover boundary in a tied match against Ipswich & East Suffolk at the ground of Tendring Park). Bill McGarry signed Joe from Millwall, and later sold him to Northampton (when they had their brief season of glory in the First Division). McGarry then bought him back again via Millwall.

Joe bought a London taxi in partnership with Pat Terry, a former Millwall striker who moved to Reading. While at cricket, he was busy learning the London streets and routes, so he could pass the examination taken by all taxi drivers before they could be granted a licence.

Joe used to collect the wicker skip, with all the shirts and boots, when Ipswich were crossing from Liverpool Street Station to another London terminal when travelling to and from away matches. The Town players used the Underground.

Joe used to buy second-hand cars from the Continent and run them on trade plates. He was always good company and attends players' reunions at Portman Road. His knees are in a poor shape these days, but he usually watches Millwall home matches from the press box, where his son works in the media. His father was a Millwall turnstile man for many years.

Joe Broadfoot, just signed from Millwall, is welcomed to Portman Road by first-team captain Andy Nelson (right). Jimmy Leadbetter, Roy Walsh, John Compton, Frank Treacy, Larry Carberry and Dennis Thrower are the other players in the picture.

Frank Brogan

Winger, 1964 to 1970

Born: Glasgow 3 August 1942
Signed: 11 June 1964, from Celtic
Debut: v. Cardiff City (away), drawn 0-0,
    22 August 1964

Ipswich career:
220 starts (3 subs), 69 goals
Football League: 201(2), 58
FA Cup: 10(1), 5
Football League Cup: 9, 6

Other clubs: Celtic and Halifax Town.

A lively left-winger signed from Celtic, Frank was playing at the time when it became fashionable for wide players to track back and help out in defence. This did not suit his style, and I recall him saying that if he spent the afternoon running up and down the touchline, how was he going to stay sharp for when the goalscoring opportunity cropped up? He was both a scorer of goals and a creator.

Brogan's expertise from the penalty spot became legendary. He missed his first attempt against Northampton Town in September 1964. He did not try again for almost two years, when he cracked the ball home against Huddersfield. This was the first of 16 successful spot kicks, including two in a match on three occasions – against Northampton Town and Millwall in the League and Colchester United in the League Cup.

Frank's talent was spotted by Jackie Milburn. He came from a footballing family, his brother Jim winning 4 caps for Scotland in 1971. Frank scored 17 goals in 1967/68 – the season Ipswich won the Second Division title under Bill McGarry – including a hat-trick in the 5-0 win over Bristol City in August. This followed on from a 7-0 victory over La Gantoise of Ghent in pre-season when Brogan scored five, the other goals coming from Danny Hegan and Colin Viljoen. This set the ball rolling for the side fashioned by Bill McGarry to win the championship, thanks to a boost given in late February by the signings of John O'Rourke and Peter Morris.

Frank was unlucky with injury in 1970. After suffering Achilles tendon problems, he then broke two bones in his foot in his comeback against Arsenal reserves. It was in this era that the Ipswich Town supporters ran their 'Blue Arrow' rail excursions to away games. There were five trips in all and the club's own relay equipment was installed on the train the night before to provide entertainment on the journey. Ipswich gained a wonderful reputation as well-behaved travelling fans, because not once was there a hint of trouble.

Brogan was a reasonable golfer with an unorthodox grip. That did not prevent him from giving me a beating round Woodbridge.

George Burley
Full-back, 1973 to 1985

Born: Cumnock 3 June 1956
Signed: 3 June 1973 from apprentice
Debut: *v.* Manchester United (away),
  29 December 1973

Ipswich career:
500 starts, 11 goals
Football League: 394, 6
FA Cup: 43, 4
Football League Cup: 35
UEFA Cup: 21
European Cup Winners' Cup: 6
FA Charity Shield: 1
Honours: 11 Scottish caps, 2 under-23 caps,
  5 under-21 caps and youth caps

Other clubs: Sunderland, Gillingham, Motherwell
  and Ayr United.

George Burley arrived as a youngster from Ayrshire, together with Kenny Taylor from the same area. He made an early impression in the youth team and Bobby Robson was quick to recognise his talent. He came through a daunting debut, marking George Best against Manchester United at Old Trafford, with his reputation enhanced: he was only 17 years and 209 days old at the time.

He played for Scotland at youth, under-23 and under-21 level before winning 11 full caps. He was in the Scottish World Cup squad in Spain in 1982.

Always a threat to the opposition going forward, he gave early indication of a cross with a windmill action with his arm. He played in the 1978 FA Cup final against Arsenal, but missed the UEFA Cup triumph in 1981 because of a serious knee injury. This was sustained in an FA Cup fourth round tie at Shrewsbury and kept him out of action for nine months. Now, when one of his players suffers cruciate ligament damage, at least he can console and encourage them by talking from experience.

Lawrie McMenemy took him to Sunderland, but he was never quite the same player on Wearside. The injury had taken its toll. He had a spell with Gillingham before a return to Scottish football with Motherwell and Ayr

United, where he was player-manager. He also had an involvement with Falkirk.

In the summer of 1994 he was appointed as player-manager of Colchester United. By Christmas he had joined Ipswich Town in somewhat acrimonious circumstances. He was under contract at Layer Road so Colchester, if they did not want to lose him, should have refused permission for Ipswich to interview him – just as Stoke City did in the case of Mick Mills way back in 1986.

Once he was told he could speak with Ipswich, it was a matter of agreeing compensation (similar to a fee for selling a player). The Ipswich chairman at the time, John Kerr, had told me that a fee had been agreed but that Colchester had come back later trying to call off the original arrangement. That's when the state of deadlock began. It was so sad to see wrangling between two excellent clubs.

Burley took Ipswich into the Premiership within the time span of the five-year plan outlined by chairman David Sheepshanks. In their first season at the top level Ipswich finished fifth and qualified for the UEFA Cup. However, the pressures of Europe, integrating new players from different cultures and a loss of confidence meant a return to the Football League the following season. This was so unexpected and so disappointing.

Terry Butcher

Defender, 1976 to 1987

Born: Singapore, 28 December 1958
Signed: 18 August 1976 from apprentice
Debut: *v.* Everton (away), lost 0-1, 15 April 1978

Ipswich career:
350 starts, 23 goals
Football League: 271, 16
FA Cup: 28
Football League: 29, 2
UEFA Cup: 20, 3
European Cup Winners Cup: 2
Honours: 77 England caps between 1980 and
    1990 (45 while at Ipswich), 7 under-21 caps.

Other clubs: Glasgow Rangers, Coventry City,
    and Sunderland.

Terry Butcher, brought up at Blundeston on the Norfolk-Suffolk border, was a 'big softie' when he first came to Portman Road as a youngster. Coach Bobby Ferguson knocked him into shape using the cruel-to-be-kind approach. Butcher's father may have disapproved at first, but the player himself went from strength to strength and ended up as captain of England.

Butcher and Russell Osman formed a central defensive barrier for Ipswich in much the same way as Allan Hunter and Kevin Beattie had done in the previous decade. Both starred in the 1980/81 UEFA Cup triumph. Had Butcher not suffered knee problems in 1985/86 season, there is little doubt that Ferguson's side would have escaped the drop. Passionate about his football, Butcher was furious when referee Gerald Ashby awarded West Ham an 86th-minute penalty, a harsh punishment for a tackle by Nigel Gleghorn. The West Ham visitors' dressing room suffered damage as a result.

Glasgow Rangers paid £725,000 for Butcher and appointed him as captain. It was a record for a Scottish club. David Pleat had been trying to

secure Butcher for Tottenham, but was reluctant to believe it when Ferguson said he had an offer of more than £700,000. Pleat had done his homework and did not think there was a club in England at the time with that sort of money. Scotland presumably was not considered.

Terry had a spell as player-manager of Coventry City, starting in November 1990. He joined Sunderland in July 1992 and had a brief spell as manager. Ferguson was coaching at Roker Park at the time. At one meeting with Sunderland supporters, which he thought was 'behind closed doors', he let it slip that he was 'as far apart from chairman Bob Murray as the banks of the Wear'. It was hardly a career-enhancing comment to make in one of football's hotbeds.

Many people still picture Butcher with his face, shirt and head bandage covered in blood. This happened in 1989 when he clashed heads with Johnny Ekstrom in a World Cup qualifier in Sweden. It looked pretty horrific, but Butcher was by then as tough as they come. He later said: 'There was no way I was going to come off with that white shirt on. It would never have entered our manager Bobby Robson's head either. He knew me well from our days at Ipswich. I also knew that if he did take me off I would probably have whacked him!'

Butcher ran a hotel at Bridge of Allan for a while, but then returned to what he knew best. He is a popular football pundit on radio and still very much involved in Scottish football.

Larry Carberry
Right-back, 1956 to 1965

Born: Liverpool 18 January 1936
Signed: 19 May 1956 when amateur
Debut: *v.* QPR (home), won 4-0, 3 November 1956

Ipswich career:
285 starts, 0 goals
Football League: 257
FA Cup: 15
Football League Cup: 8
European Cup: 2
FA Charity Shield: 1
Other matches: 2

Other club: Barrow.

One of five Town footballers with championship medals in the top three divisions, Carberry took over from the late Basil Acres as the regular right-back. He won his place in the first team only a few months after joining the club as an amateur from the Army. Acres had been captain in most matches that autumn, and the role was taken by centre-half Doug Rees. Once in the side, the stylish Carberry was there to stay.

Carberry had an unusual entry into the world of professional football. His father was employed in Liverpool docks and insisted that his son was apprenticed as a sheet-metal worker after finishing his schooling at St Anthony's Roman Catholic School. When he was eighteen, he went on tour with Liverpool Boys' Association in Holland and Germany. On his return he was signed on amateur forms by Everton, but it was not long before he was called up for National Service. He was posted to Trieste with the Lancashire Fusiliers. Later he was transferred to the King's Regiment and towards the end of his time as a soldier he was stationed at Bury St Edmunds. Alf Ramsey spotted him in an Army match against Bury Town. He signed for Ipswich first as an amateur and then accepted professional terms after interest had been shown by Norwich City and Liverpool. In fact he was offered a trial at Anfield, but did not bother to make the trip to Merseyside.

Speed was one of Carberry's greatest assets. He was chosen as a reserve for the England under-23 side to meet Romania at Wembley. He also represented the Football Association in matches against the Army and the RAF. He came very close to an own goal in the final match of the Championship season against Villa, the report reading: 'Baker slipped a ball through for Dougan and Carberry very nearly put though his own goal, the ball passing just wide of the post'.

Carberry, who damaged his ribs in a car accident, left Ipswich to join Barrow in July 1965. Later he was involved with non-League Burscough. He spent nineteen years with Liverpool Maritime Terminals until being made redundant in August 1989. His other sporting interests used to include swimming, table-tennis and crown green bowls.

Tommy Carroll

Right-back, 1966 to 1971

Born: Dublin, 18 August 1942
Signed: 9 July 1966 from Cambridge City for £1,500
Debut: v. Hull City (away), drawn 1-1,
    18 March 1967

Ipswich career:
124 starts (2 subs), 3 goals
Football League: 115 (2), 2 goals
FA Cup: 2
Football League Cup: 7, 1
Honours: 17 caps for the Republic of Ireland (8 of
    them while with Ipswich)

Other clubs: Shelbourne, Cambridge City and
    Birmingham City.

Bill McGarry's scouting network picked up Irishman Tommy Carroll at non-League Cambridge City. It took the Dubliner a few months to acclimatise to full-time League football. He made his debut at Hull in March 1967. He came in at right-back, looked the part and established himself not only at Ipswich but in the Republic of Ireland team as well. His chance arose when Mick McNeil, so unlucky with injuries that season, was ruled out by a car accident.

The arrival of Bobby Robson as Ipswich manager, after McGarry moved to Wolves, led to gradually increasing dressing-room friction between Bill Baxter, Carroll and the manager – who felt he needed to establish his authority. After what Robson described as a row over a 'minor issue', Carroll went home to Dublin and was duly suspended.

The big rift came when Carroll and his friend Bill Baxter, together with their wives, found themselves barred from the players' lounge after a match in which they were not playing. Robson had pinned a notice on the dressing-room noticeboard stating that only players in the team that day could use the facility. Carroll stormed into the dressing room, tore down the notice in front of Robson's eyes and screwed up the paper. This was watched by the other players. They all wondered what would happen next. Robson regarded his noticeboard, which also included the team sheet, as sacrosanct. He knew this was a big test of his management skills. It turned into an unseemly brawl. Carroll and Robson clashed. Baxter joined in on Carroll's side and coach Cyril Lea helped Robson.

The players concerned had to leave the club, there was no question about that. Carroll was sold to Birmingham City for £20,000 and Baxter to Hull City for £12,000. Dressing-room problems spring up all the time in football, many unpublicised. Just remember how Roy Keane, the Republic of Ireland's dominating captain, left the rest of his 2002 World Cup squad in Japan after giving coach Mick McCarthy unacceptable verbal abuse.

Although it was sad for Ipswich to lose two excellent players, the dressing-room atmosphere improved as a result. The remaining senior players sent a short statement to the Press saying that they backed Robson and wanted to see an end to all the unrest. Carroll was a skilled carpet-layer. He was also a quality footballer whose career was ended by an ankle injury.

Frank Clarke
Centre forward, 1970 to 1973

Born: Willenhall 15 July 1942
Signed: 14 March 1970 from QPR for £40,000
Debut: *v.* Sunderland (home), won 2-0,
    21 March 1970

Ipswich career:
71 starts (5 subs), 17 games
Football League: 62(4), 15
FA Cup: 6, 2
Football League Cup: 3
Texaco Cup: (1)

Other clubs: QPR, Shrewsbury Town and
    Carlisle United.

Although he had a comparatively short spell at Ipswich, Frank Clarke's first seven matches helped lift the club clear of relegation. This was vital to Bobby Robson's career and set the club on the path to glory, both domestically and in Europe.

Clarke was the eldest of footballing brothers. Allan, nicknamed 'Sniffer', played for Leeds United and England. Then there were Wayne and Derek. Frank left Ipswich to join Carlisle for £36,000 in August 1973, so Ipswich recouped most of their initial outlay. The Cumbrian club was then in the First Division and Frank scored a goal in their shock 2-1 victory over Ipswich at Brunton Park. Another Town old boy, Eddie Spearritt, was also in the Carlisle side that day.

On his retirement from football, Frank ran a newsagents' shop and then became supervisor at a sports centre.

John Colrain

Forward, 1963 to 1966

Born: Glasgow, 4 February 1937
Died: July 1984
Signed: 23 May 1963 from Clyde
Debut: v. Everton (home), drawn 0-0,
    14 September 1963

Ipswich career:
61 starts (one sub), 20 goals
Football League: 55(1), 20
Football League Cup: 6, 3
Honours: 1 Scottish under-23 cap before
    joining Ipswich

Other clubs: Celtic, Clyde, Glentoran and
    St Patrick's Athletic.

They called him 'Big Coley' in the dressing room or 'Hoss' on the terraces. He was certainly a leader amongst the growing Scottish contingent at Portman Road. He had played for Celtic and Scotland's under-23 team. Many of the other lads – the impressionable ones – looked up to him. As to whether he always led them in the direction the manager wanted was very much open to question. He was heavily built and none-too-fast, but had a cannonball shot with either foot.

One thing was certain, John enjoyed a busy social life. I recall travelling with the Ipswich party to an away match against Birmingham City in September 1963. It was only Colrain's third League match for the club and one assumed he would be keen to impress. The team travelled by train and stayed at an hotel in the city centre. After dinner I was sitting in the lounge drinking coffee and brandy with chairman John Cobbold, trainer Jimmy Forsyth and manager Jackie Milburn. The players had all gone to bed for the night – or at least that's what Milburn believed.

'Mr John', as the chairman was known, then said: 'Jimmy, just go and check that all the players are in their rooms'. There was a protest from Milburn that the chairman should doubt the professionalism of his squad. 'Mr John', however, insisted that the check went ahead. He had obviously spotted a couple of the lads slipping out of the hotel. Sure enough, Forsyth returned with the news that Colrain and Bill Baxter were missing.

A reception committee (those round the table) awaited the return of the two players until the early hours of the morning. Asked what they had been doing, the astonishing reply was: 'Playing gramophone records with Bertie Auld'. Auld was a former Celtic colleague of Colrain's who was then on Birmingham City's injury list. Milburn was astounded. He faced the problem of how to deal with the situation in the best interests of the club. Should he send both players home in disgrace and face all sorts of damaging publicity or should he take a lenient view because he needed both of them for a vital match at St Andrew's? Both lads played that afternoon. Ipswich lost 1-0 and Milburn wasted an opportunity to impose his authority.

Colrain became player-manager of Glentoran, with whom he won two Irish League titles and lost to Benfica on away goals in the European Cup. He left after a failing to agree fresh terms and joined St Patrick's Athletic as a player. Later he scouted for Manchester City and Partick Thistle. Sadly, he died young.

John Compton
Left-back, 1960 to 1963

Born: Poplar, 27 August 1937
Signed: 27 July 1960 from Chelsea
Debut: *v.* Luton Town (away), lost 2-3,
    5 November 1960

Ipswich career:
131 starts, 0 goals
Football League: 111
FA Cup: 10
Football League Cup: 6
European Cup: 3
FA Charity Shield: 1

Other clubs: Chelsea and Bournemouth.

John Compton came to Portman Road as a wing-half from Chelsea in 1960. The London club were looking for a £4,000 transfer fee, but Ipswich paid considerably less. He played three matches in the Second Division promotion campaign, his debut at Luton on 5 November being something of a damp squib with a 3-2 defeat. He was in a losing team at Portsmouth, but played his part in a home win against Huddersfield.

He came into his own in the late summer of 1961 when Ken Malcolm was ruled out by injury. Compton was switched from wing-half to left-back, an inspirational decision by Alf Ramsey. He passed his first examination with flying colours when he tamed Burnley and England winger John Connelly – a match-winner on his day. Ipswich won that game 6-2 against the club destined to be runners-up in the title race.

Compton went on to make 55 successive first-team appearances and became well established. He stayed as a regular for two more seasons until joining Bournemouth in June 1964. He made way for the arrival of Mick McNeil, an England international, from Middlesbrough. Compton never scored a goal for Ipswich, but he should have done. At the start of 1963/64, Ted Phillips had two penalties against Manchester United saved by Harry Gregg. Towards the end of that season, Ipswich were awarded a third spot-kick against Leicester City at Filbert Street. This time Compton shouldered the responsibility but Gordon Banks brought off a save.

Compton was the son of a London docker who had played as an amateur with Millwall and encouraged his boys to play football. John did not let his father down. He captained Cornwell Secondary Modern and Essex Schoolboys. He joined Dagenham at the age of sixteen and subsequently became a member of the Chelsea ground staff. He almost became a Charlton player after an invitation to a trial at The Valley.

He made his First Division debut for Chelsea at Blackpool while on National Service in the RAMC who were, very conveniently, based at Woolwich. He was chosen to play for the Army against Aston Villa, but had to withdraw because of flu. Perhaps the least known member of Ramsey's Championship-winning side, there is no doubt that he played an important role. He has worked as a petrol tanker driver for Texaco in recent years.

Paul Cooper

Goalkeeper, 1974 to 1987

Born: Brierley Hill 21 December 1953
Signed: 18 June 1974 from Birmingham City
    for £23,000
Debut: *v.* Leeds United (away), lost 2-3,
    20 April 1974

Ipswich career:
575 starts
Football League: 447
Play-offs: 2
FA Cup; 45
Football League Cup: 43
UEFA Cup: 28
European Cup Winners' Cup: 6
FA Charity Shield: 1
Full Members' Cup: 3

Other clubs: Birmingham City, Leicester City,
    Manchester City and Stockport County.

In the 1979/80 season he saved five out of seven.

He played in an FA Cup semi-final for Birmingham City as a youngster, but when he first arrived in Suffolk he could not displace the daring Laurie Sivell. Once Cooper became established he served the club with distinction, both domestically and in Europe. After he moved to Leicester he invited me to play golf at Luffenham Heath. I was hardly expecting to find an informal tournament that included Gary McAllister and Steve Walsh as well as snooker player Willie Thorne. It turned into an entertaining day (and night).

Ipswich Town used to make regular use of the Stamford George Hotel for a meal on return trips from the North on a Saturday night. The party had a room to themselves. On one occasion, manager Bobby Ferguson stayed in the North East to see his family after a match at Sunderland. A bit of a fracas took place after one of the players joked: 'What is green and can't catch a cross?' You can probably imagine the scene. Ipswich Town have not stopped at Stamford since. Now, of course, they have cooking facilities on the team coach.

Cooper now lives in Tenerife running a business organising tee times for tourists and hotel guests on local golf courses.

Paul Cooper became famed for saving penalties. One day he told me that his secret was simple. He would stand fractionally nearer to one post than the other, thus offering the penalty taker an obviously larger target. He hoped it would be considered a double bluff. He would then make the shortest dive giving himself a better chance of bringing off the save if the penalty taker had fallen for the ruse. As to whether this was the entire truth or just what he cared to tell me after a successful day at Newmarket races is another matter. His penalty-saving record was 19 from 49 kicks over a fourteen-year period. In his final season at Portman Road, he saved six out of eleven.

Ian Cranson
Defender, 1982 to 1988

Born: Easington, 2 July 1964
Signed: 2 July 1982 from apprentice
Debut: v. Aston Villa (away), lost 0-4,
    17 December 1983

Ipswich career:
162 starts (2 subs), 5 goals
Football League: 130(1), 5
FA Cup: 11, (1)
Football League Cup: 15
Full Members' Cup: 7
Honours: 5 England under-21 caps

Other clubs: Sheffield Wednesday and Stoke City.

Ian Cranson was another brilliant defender to come off the production line at Portman Road. Sadly for him the glory years were over, but he was one of the toughest tacklers I can ever remember. A challenge at Boothferry Park sticks in my mind: it was perfectly fair but play was held up for some considerable time before the Hull City attacker recovered.

Cranson scored a cracking goal against Southampton at Portman Road in August 1985. Jason Dozzell played the ball into his path from a corner taken by Mark Brennan. It was cheered by the lowest crowd at Portman Road for twenty-one years (11,588). What was wrong with the Town fans that day? It was First Division fare and they could not all have had the excuse that they were gathering in the harvest.

Ever present in 1985/86 season, he joined Sheffield Wednesday for £450,000 in March 1988. Mick Mills signed him for Stoke City for £480,000 in July 1989, after which he overcame two serious knee operations. He often wore a distinctive head-band to protect an old injury.

Ian Cranson at the ready with Steve Whitton, then a Birmingham City player, in close attention.

Ray Crawford
Centre forward, 1958 to 1963 and 1966 to 1969

Born: Portsmouth 13 July 1937
Signed: 6 September 1958 from Portsmouth
Debut: v. Swansea Town (away), lost 2-4,
   4 October 1958

Ipswich career:
354 starts, 228 goals
Football League: 320, 204
FA Cup: 18, 5
Football League Cup: 10, 10
European Cup: 4, 8
FA Charity Shield: 1, 0
Other matches: 1, 1
Honours: 2 full England caps v. Northern Ireland
   and Austria in 1962. 2 Football League
   appearances

Other League clubs: Portsmouth, Wolverhampton
   Wanderers, West Bromwich, Charlton
   Athletic, Kettering Town, and Colchester
   United. (He then moved to South Africa.)

Ray Crawford arrived at Ipswich not long after completing his National Service in Malaya, which is why he was nicknamed 'Jungle Boy'. The son of a professional boxer, his schoolmaster tried to discourage him from becoming a footballer. Fortunately, the advice was ignored.

Along with Derek Kevan of West Bromwich, he was joint leading marksman in Ipswich Town's First Division Championship-winning season. When he joined Ipswich for a reported £5,000 fee, he found himself trying to step into the boots of the popular Tom Garneys. Crawford started with two goals on his debut at Swansea – where the inmates of the nearby prison can watch football at Vetch Field from their roof. Ipswich, though, lost 4-2. Later that season, Ray scored his first hat-trick for his new club when Swansea came to Portman Road at the end of February. Ipswich won 3-2.

Many of Ray's goals came from within the six-yard box. He could sniff out the half-chance and latched onto rebounds from the fierce long-range shooting of Ted Phillips. Ray's second Ipswich hat-trick was scored at Brighton in a 5-2 win during the club's Second Division title triumph under Alf Ramsey. He also scored three at Elland Road in a 5-2 win over Leeds.

Even the defences of the First Division could not contain Crawford in those days, with a hat-trick over Sheffield Wednesday at Hillsborough in a 3-0 win. He also scored five in the club's record 10-0 victory over Floriana of Malta in the European Cup.

Crawford holds the distinction of scoring a hat-trick in the Football League, the League Cup, the FA Cup and the European Cup. He scored in seven successive League and League Cup games between 17 August and 7 September in 1968. This feat was equalled by Marcus Stewart with a run that started on Boxing Day 2000.

Ipswich were relegated with 25 points from 42 matches (two points for a win and one for a draw) in 1963/64, but Crawford could not be blamed. He was sold to Wolverhampton Wanderers, which left such a gaping hole that Town tried five different centre forwards in the next 14 matches. Just for the record, they were: Bobby Blackwood, John Colrain, Doug Moran, Ted Phillips and Frank Treacy.

In December, Ipswich signed Gerry Baker from Hibernian for a Town record £17,000 to try to solve the problem. In the meantime, Crawford scored 39 goals in 57 games for Wolves before a less successful move to West Bromwich, where he played only 14 matches before Bill McGarry brought him back to Ipswich in March 1966.

People say it's seldom a good idea to retrace your steps, but Crawford proved to be the exception to the rule. Although Ted Phillips was no longer there, he soon formed a good understanding with players like Baker, Frank Brogan and Danny Hegan. He did not miss a single match in the 1966/67 season and the following year won another Second Division Championship medal and had the satisfaction of scoring four goals against Southampton in a 5-2 Football League Cup first round victory.

Crawford departed early in the reign of Bobby Robson. A few matches with Charlton were followed by a leading role in Colchester United's most glorious hour, when they performed one of the giant-killing acts of the century to knock Don Revie's all-conquering Leeds United out of the FA Cup at Layer Road in 1971. The U's won 3-2 and Crawford scored twice.

Some non-League football with Kettering and a spell in South Africa with Durban City preceded Ray's return to England. He held posts as youth coach at Brighton and Portsmouth and managed Fareham Town. Ray must number amongst the most popular players ever to wear an Ipswich shirt.

Born: Wimbledon 12 November 1969
Signed: 29 October 1996 on loan from
    Tottenham Hotspur
Debut: v. Southend United (home), drawn 1-1,
    9 November 1996

Ipswich career:
68 starts (4 subs), 3 goals
Football League and play-offs: 56(4), 3
FA Cup: 4
Football League Cup: 8
Honours: 3 caps for England under-21 while
    with Chelsea

Other clubs: Chelsea, Tottenham, Crystal Palace
    (loan), Bristol City (loan) and Portsmouth.

A wholehearted defender, Jason Cundy seemed to be one of the bargains of the season when he joined Ipswich from Tottenham in November 1996. He overcame the problem of having to play alongside three different central defensive partners in his the first few weeks (Steve Sedgley, Adam Tanner and Chris Swailes). Then came the chilling news that he had been diagnosed with testicular cancer. It was something the club understandably concealed for as long as possible to prevent extra pressure on his family. When

he had made a complete recovery, he worked hard to raise awareness of the need for early detection of this disease.

Before the start of 1998/99 season, he damaged his ankle when skipping to get fit. He made only one start that campaign and then moved to Portsmouth where his career was further jinxed by injury.

He began his career with Chelsea as a trainee. He played 41 League games before a £750,000 move to Tottenham after a loan spell at White Hart Lane. He played only 16 League games for Spurs, where a bad injury kept him out of contention for eighteen months. Replacements were signed and, when he was fit again, Ossie Ardiles never really gave him a chance. Then Gerry Francis took over and was straight to the point. Cundy was told he did not feature in future plans.

While at Spurs, Cundy scored one of the most bizarre goals ever seen at Portman Road. In a match during the 1992/93 season he went into a challenge with David Linighan near the halfway line. The ball rocketed away, assisted by the wind, and looped over the head of Craig Forrest who was off his line in the goal at the North Stand end.

Cundy's wife Lizzie, a model, had a bit-part as a waitress in a nightclub, in the James Bond movie, *Tomorrow Never Dies*.

Loan spells at Crystal Palace and then Bristol City preceded his move to Portman Road.

Mich D'Avray
Forward, 1979 to 1990

Born: Johannesburg 19 February 1962
Signed: 9 May 1979 from apprentice
Debut: *v.* Southampton (home), won 3-1,
    24 November 1979

Ipswich career:
201 starts (54 subs), 45 goals
Football League: 170(41), 37
Play-offs: (2)
FA Cup: 9(2), 2
Football League Cup: 19(4), 5
UEFA Cup: 1, (2)
Full Members' Cup: 2(3), 1
Honours: 2 England under-21 caps

Other clubs: NEC Nijmegen and Leicester (loan).

Mich D'Avray came from South Africa on the recommendation of former player Colin Viljoen. It took him four years to secure a British passport, after which he won 2 caps for the England under-21 side, taking over from Mark Hateley. He had a loan spell at Leicester when Bryan Hamilton was manager at Filbert Street.

Often used as a substitute, he was a regular in the team that reached the semi-finals of the Milk Cup in 1985, only to lose to Norwich City in the second leg at Carrow Road. He scored five goals in that run, but suffered a nasty injury against the Canaries. In a clash with central defender Dave Watson he swallowed his tongue. It was just as well that referee Keith Hackett realised what had happened and came to the rescue.

Mich had a spell with NEC Nijmegen in Holland before returning to coach the Olympic team in South Africa. Then he coached Cape Town Spurs and won the Tony Naidoo Cape Soccer Personality of the Year award and the Matt Busby Memorial award for being coach of the year. More recently he took a post with Perth Glory in Western Australia.

Jason Dozzell

Inside forward, 1984 to 1992 and 1998

Born: Ipswich, 9 December 1967
Signed: 21 December 1984 from apprentice
Debut: *v.* Coventry City (home), won 3-1,
    4 February 1984

Ipswich career:
394 starts (21 subs), 71 goals
Premiership: 41, 7
Football League: 279(20), 46
Play-offs: 2
FA Cup: 22, 12
Football League Cup: 30(1), 4
Full Members' Cup: 20, 2
Honours: 9 England under-21 caps.

Other clubs: Tottenham Hotspur, Northampton
    Town and Colchester United

Jason Dozzell, still a pupil at Chantry High School in Ipswich, was given a pat on the back by manager Bobby Ferguson and sent on the field as a substitute against Coventry City at Portman Road. He was only 16 years and 57 days old and in the 89th minute became the youngest player ever to score in the First Division.

It was clear from the start that Dozzell possessed immense natural talent. He was aware of everything going on around him; his vision was fantastic. Ferguson was a manager who liked to give young players the chance, but the public were not responding and there were only 13,406 in the ground for Dozzell's historic debut.

Dozzell played under Ferguson, John Duncan and John Lyall and looked to be an England star in the making. He broke into the England under-21 side but rather blotted his copy book out in Toulon. Together with Ipswich colleague Mark Brennan and Norwich City pair Dale Gordon and Robert Rosario, he broke a curfew imposed by coach Dave Sexton. It was dawn when they returned to the hotel, leaping from yacht to yacht on the quayside. Dozzell fell in and there was quite a commotion because he could not swim. Sexton had a bedroom overlooking the water, heard the noise and looked out of the window. He saw everything and the Toulon four found themselves in disgrace.

Dozzell was a hero in the Press box at Millwall at the start of February 1992. We had heard that he was being switched into attack. The bookmakers thought he was staying in midfeld and offered 16-1 against him scoring the first goal. After 33 minutes Dozzell found the net. Many of the journalists had some sort of financial interest and I was delegated to collect more than £700 during the interval to be

Jason Dozzell gets a pat on the back from experienced goalkeeper Paul Cooper and the adulation of young fans as he leaves the field after becoming the youngest player ever to score in the First Division. Mark Brennan, also a teenager, is on the right of the picture.

shared out. I must admit I felt a little uneasy picking up that sort of money and having to make my way through a Millwall crowd back to the Press box. Ipswich went on to win 3-2, their first League success at Millwall for thirty-six years.

Dozzell's sale to Tottenham for £1.9 million was one of those deals that enabled Ipswich to keep their books balanced, although everyone was sorry to see him go. It is always pleasing when a local boy makes good. London life did not seem to suit Dozzell, who never really made the impact everyone expected at White Hart Lane. In the 1997/98 season he had a brief spell back at Portman Road under George Burley, but was not offered a long-term contract. He

helped Town reach the quarter-finals of the Coca Cola Cup by scoring the opening goal in the 2-1 extra-time victory at Oxford United in the fourth round.

If Dozzell's talent had been allied to Mick Stockwell's determination, then what a player he would have been. His potential was largely unfulfilled. He ended his playing days with Colchester United, where a toe injury forced his premature retirement from League football.

An incident he may never forget was when his half brother, Tony Swallow, ran onto the pitch at Carrow Road and planted a blue-and-white hat on Jason's head. Tony had wrongly anticipated the final whistle and was arrested but, happily, the fine was minimal.

Kieron Dyer

Midfield, 1996 to 1998

It was always evident that Kieron was something special, though he is far from robust and some felt he might be too small to become a successful professional. They thought the same about Kevin Keegan. His assets are quick feet and a sharp footballing brain. Kieron must be the most famous old boy from Westbourne High School in Ipswich.

He was thrown in at the deep end when Ipswich were drawn away to Nottingham Forest in the third round of the FA Cup, where he had his first start. He was selected on the opposite side of the field to Stuart Pearce, one of the tougher tacklers of his era. He proved his toughness when he scored a goal against Watford at Portman Road with a broken leg in 1998. He recalls: 'At the start

Born: Ipswich, 29 December 1978
Signed: 3 January 1997 from YTS
Debut: v. Crystal Palace (home), won 3-1,
    26 December 1996

Ipswich career:
100 starts (14 subs), 12 goals
Football League: 79(13), 9
Play-offs: 5(1), 2
FA Cup: 5
Football League Cup: 11, 1
Honours: Full England international in World Cup squad 2002, B international, under-21 and
    youth caps

Other club: Newcastle United.

Kieron Dyer takes advice from coach Stewart Houston.

Kieron Dyer, in a Newcastle United shirt, tugs at the shirt of Mark Venus as the Ipswich defender carries the ball upfield.

of the game I was on the receiving end of a couple of bad tackles. I just thought I'd got a bit of a knock that I'd be able to run off. Then I scored a goal and, although my leg was still hurting, I wanted to see out the rest of the game.'

It became clear before long that he had a bigger problem than he imagined. An X-ray showed a cracked fibula and part of his recovery was done in an oxygen chamber.

He was called into the England squad by Glenn Hoddle just before the present Tottenham manager resigned. Hoddle, according to his assistant John Gorman, planned to give Dyer a taste of the big time. The cautious Howard Wilkinson had been given temporary charge, so gambles like that were out of the question.

Dyer moved to Newcastle United for £6 million with a sell-on clause. The money was able to help fund Ipswich's successful promotion bid in 1999/2000. Had he stayed at Portman Road, Ipswich might have been tempted to channel too many of their attacks through him and thus become too predictable.

Dyer has won over fans on Tyneside with his skill. If he can steer clear of injury he can become one of the superstars of the game.

John Elsworthy

Inside left and left half, 1949 to 1965

Born: Nantyderry, Wales 26 July 1931
Date signed: 9 May 1949 when amateur at
  Newport County
Debut: *v.* Notts County (home), lost 0-4,
  27 December 1949

Ipswich career:
435 starts, 53 goals
Football League: 398, 45
FA Cup: 27, 7
Football League Cup: 6
European Cup: 3, 1
FA Charity Shield: 1
Other match: 1

Only one player in the history of the Football League has won two Third Division (South), one Second Division and one First Division championship medal. That is John Elsworthy. How on earth the Welsh selectors never awarded him a cap is beyond belief. Perhaps it was because he played for a club that was, at the time, considered to be unfashionable.

It's not that Wales were unaware. They picked 'Big John' in their twenty-two for the World Cup in Sweden in 1958. His name is still officially listed in the squad and can be

found on the FIFA World Cup internet site. Unfortunately, the Welsh FA were short of funds at the time and reduced their travelling party to eighteen at the last moment.

John started as an inside left under Scott Duncan. He made his Town debut in a 4-0 home defeat at the hands of Notts County in an Ipswich team that finished that season only three points away from having to seek re-election. The side that took the field on that occasion was: Tom Brown, Alec Mitchell, Vic Snell, Harry Baird (captain), George Clarke, Tommy Parker, Jackie Brown, John Gibbons, George Perrett, Bill Jennings, John Elsworthy and Joe O'Brien.

Times changed for the better at Portman Road, although it was not until 1952/53 season that Elsworthy became established in the side.

Elsworthy's form in the FA Cup at the start of 1953 attracted scouts to Portman Road, despite the road links being so slow. He scored the equaliser against Bradford City (including England and Yorkshire cricketer Brian Close) at Valley Parade to earn a replay, which Ipswich won 5-1. The next task was a third round tie against Everton at Goodison Park in one of the few seasons the Merseyside club has not graced the top division.

Elsworthy gave an eye-catching display that led to interest from Liverpool. This cooled in the following weeks when Elsworthy lost form and was given a brief run in the reserves.

It was in 1955 that he made the switch from inside left to left half and became such a dominant force in the side. Tommy Parker moved up into attack and started to hammer in the goals.

In October 1955 he was a reserve for the Third Division (South) against Third Division (North) at Accrington. In 1956/57 he represented the South against the North in matches at Coventry and Stockport.

In the year Ipswich won the First Division title at the first attempt, Elsworthy helped break the deadlock in the final match of the season at home to Aston Villa. It was looking like stalemate with Ipswich showing signs of nerves. Then, in the 72nd minute, Elsworthy moved into the Villa penalty area with Roy Stephenson about to swing in a free-kick from near the right touchline. Elsworthy's header rebounded off the crossbar, leaving Ray Crawford to fling himself forward to head past goalkeeper Nigel Sims and into the net.

It was a magical moment for Ipswich fans, made even better four minutes later when Ray Crawford beat Villa central defender John Sleeuwenhoek to a long ball forward. He made it 2-0 after a run of forty yards. Then came the news that Chelsea, already relegated, had forced a 1-1 draw with Burnley at Turf Moor and Ipswich were celebrating the title in style.

Elsworthy's only goal in the European Cup came in the record-breaking 10-0 victory over Floriana of Malta, who were later coached by Ted Phillips. Elsworthy ran a grocery business in Foxhall Road in Ipswich while he was still a player. Even in those days, this was unusual. He overcame his share of injuries, including two cartilage operations (long before keyhole surgery), a broken jaw and an attack of thrombosis.

A useful cricketer in his younger days, he was offered trials by Glamorgan as a fast bowler. He went to a rugby-playing school and started his football with Corporation Road Youth Club in Newport, for whom he played as an amateur. His first job was as a sixteen-year-old British Railways clerk working in Cardiff. His son, Martin, is head professional at Rookery Park Golf Club, near Lowestoft.

Born: Vancouver 20 September 1967
Signed: 31 August 1985 from apprentice
Debut: *v.* Stoke City, away, drawn 1-1,
 27 August 1988

Ipswich career:
312 starts
Premiership: 74
Football League: 189
FA Cup: 14
Football League Cup: 21
Anglo-Italian Cup: 3
Full Members' Cup: 11
Honours: Capped 56 times by Canada

Other clubs: Colchester United and West Ham.

The 6ft 4in Canadian had an excellent season when Ipswich won promotion into the Premiership under John Lyall. He was commanding in the air, although his kicking was always a cause for concern. This was perhaps because he played ice hockey as a youngster and never really became involved with outfield play at football. It became even more of a worry after 'keepers were barred from handling backpasses.

Supporters voted him their Player of the Year in the disastrous relegation season of 1994/95, despite having to pick the ball out of his net nine times against Manchester United at Old Trafford. Even that day he brought off many fine saves that prevented an even worse rout.

In that season, 'Ipswich Town nil' was a fairly predictable scoreline. It was a potential winner to back the correct score on the fixed odds taking in defeats of four, five, six and seven; it was three at the interval in Manchester that day. Who could have predicted nine?

The fact that Craig was Canada's first-choice goalkeeper meant lengthy trips away on international duty. The emergence of Richard Wright led to Forrest becoming second choice, so he took the opportunity to join West Ham United. There he found himself as understudy to Ludo Miklosko, Shaka Hislop and David James. In the year

2001 he was diagnosed with testicular cancer. He had early treatment and, like Jason Cundy, has been keen to do all he can to make people aware of this particular problem. The quicker the treatment starts, the better the chance of success.

Craig hits a golf ball a prodigious distance, but sometimes his direction is lacking by a few degrees. It can be expensive on balls.

As a youngster he was recommended to Ipswich by former Town player Phil Trenter. He paid his own air fare to England, confident that he could make the grade. It was a gamble that paid off handsomely.

Now he has retired from football on medical advice. He had his first experience of media work on Canadian television during the 2002 World Cup.

Tom Garneys

Centre forward, 1951 to 1959

'Give it to Garneys' was the cry from the Portman Road terraces way back in the 1950s. One of the most popular players ever to wear an Ipswich Town shirt, he scored 143 goals in 274 games: that averages better than a goal every second game.

A Londoner, he was one of the unlucky ones whose football career was put on hold by the Second World War. He was twenty-five years old by the time he signed for Notts County after playing for Leytonstone. There was limited opportunity for a striker at Meadow Lane in those days when the great Tommy Lawton was still scoring freely – Lawton played in Town's 2-9 defeat at Notts County in 1948, when he scored four times.

Garneys returned to London to join Brentford in December 1949 and scored a couple of goals in a dozen first-team appearances, but he had done enough to catch the eye of shrewd Ipswich Town boss Scott Duncan. Once at Portman Road, the career of Tom Garneys started to blossom, even though he was a week short of his twenty-eighth birthday. At first he formed a successful partnership with Sammy McCrory, who went on to win international honours for Northern Ireland (a better team then than they are now) after leaving Portman Road.

Ipswich reached the third round of the FA Cup in the 1951/52 season, when they played two draws with Gateshead. The matter was settled in a second replay on the neutral venue of Bramall Lane in Sheffield, which was still one of Yorkshire County Cricket Club's main home grounds. Garneys scored as Ipswich went out to the North Eastern club 2-1.

In 1952, Ipswich sold McCrory to Plymouth Argyle for £5,000 and parted with Allenby Driver and Jimmy Roberts as well. They found themselves desperately short of goals, the problem becoming acute when Garneys missed the final quarter of the season with a serious back injury. Scott Duncan solved the problems for the following season when he secured the services of two excellent wingers, Billy Reed from Brighton and George McLuckie from Blackburn Rovers. They also signed Alec Crowe, an inside-right from St Mirren.

Born: Leyton, 25 April 1923
Signed: 25 May 1951 from Brentford
Debut: v. Southend, home, won 4-1, 18 August 1951

Ipswich career:
274 starts, 143 goals
Football League: 248, 123
FA Cup: 25, 20
Other Match: 1

Previous clubs: Notts County and Brentford.

This turned out to be a promotion season in which Garneys played his part to the full with 19 goals in the Third Division (South) as well as seven in an FA Cup run that started to put the club on the football map. Garneys scored in the 4-1 win over Reading in the first round, but then it took two games to overcome the amateurs (or were they shamateurs?) of Walthamstow Avenue. The Avenue had thirty-four-year-old Stan Gerula in goal. He was a Polish wartime international who doubled up as groundsman at Walthamstow. Ipswich found themselves two down at home. Then Neil Myles netted from the penalty spot before Tom Brown forced a replay in London which Town won with an 86th-minute goal from Crowe, who had been left out of the first game. In the third round, Oldham Athletic, at that time bottom of the Second Division, came to Portman Road under control of their player-manager George Hardwick, whose statue stands outside the Riverside Stadium at Middlesbrough. It was 3-3 at Portman Road. In the replay at Boundary Park, Town goal-keeper Jack Parry, who had taken some criticism in the first match, gave a breathtaking display. Hardwick missed a penalty and Garneys grabbed the winner.

Ipswich then beat Birmingham City – a notable scalp – 1-0. The visitors included England goalkeeper Gil Merrick. The second-half commentary was broadcast on BBC radio. Ipswich met their match in the fifth round against Preston North End at Deepdale. It was 6-1 to one of the top teams in the land that was able to field Tom Finney in his prime, Tommy Docherty and Charlie Wayman in a star-studded side. Ipswich struggled with nine men for 15 minutes while Basil Acres and Doug Rees were off for repairs. During that time, Preston scored their third and fourth goals. Garneys was the Ipswich marksman.

Ipswich managed just one season in the Second Division, despite a great 6-1 victory over Doncaster Rovers at the end of October when Garneys scored four times. He also scored twice in early season games at home to Luton Town and Middlesbrough. I saw both those games in the school holidays and remember names like Bernard Streten in goal for Luton and Jesse Pye up front. Boro had Rolando Ugolini in goal.

Scott Duncan handed over to Alf Ramsey. Garneys stayed in the forefront, setting up a splendid partnership with Tommy Parker, who scored 30 goals in the League thanks to the openings the wily Garneys created. He scored 19 himself with Wilf Grant collecting 16. Ipswich missed promotion by a couple of points. Town went up the following season, towards the end of which Ipswich appointed twenty-nine-year-old John Cobbold as chairman in succession to his cousin Alistair.

Garneys was top Ipswich scorer in the Second Division in the 1957/58 season of consolidation. The following campaign he played in the first four League matches before handing over the number nine shirt to Dermot Curtis, who soon became the second player to win a full cap while an Ipswich player, being selected for the Republic of Ireland versus Poland on 5 October.

Garneys became landlord of the Mulberry Tree pub in Ipswich before retiring to live in Billericay.

Tom Garneys is the player on the left of this trio of Town players, the others being John Elsworthy and George McLuckie.

Born: Ferryhill, 26 June 1955
Signed: 24 October 1972 from apprentice
Debut: *v.* Wolverhampton Wanderers (home),
   won 2-0, 27 October 1973

Ipswich career:
345 starts (39 subs), 96 goals
Football League: 267(29), 73
FA Cup: 26(3), 8
Football League Cup: 28(1), 8
UEFA Cup: 21(5), 5
European Cup Winners' Cup: 2(1), 2
FA Charity Shield: 1
Honours: Twice capped by England in 1981

Other clubs: Sunderland and Carlisle United.
   Coach at Hartlepool.

How many times, in the present climate of refereeing, would Gates be shown the yellow card for diving? He operated just behind the strikers and was brave enough to accept the ball to feet and try to turn defenders in the penalty area. He was always confident of his own ability, which led to problems with manager Bobby Robson.

Gates felt that his first-team chance was not coming quickly enough, so he returned to the North East in protest. He was said to be potato-picking. He hoped to press Robson into promising him a first-team place. Instead, he earned himself a suspension and a fine. There was deadlock, which was eventually broken by the intervention and advice of PFA secretary Cliff Lloyd.

Gates' elder brother, Bill, played at centre-half for Middlesbrough and became a successful businessman – although no relation to the computer man of the same name in the United States. Town coach Bobby Ferguson championed Gates' cause at Portman Road and it was not before long that he became an automatic choice.

Those who watched Ipswich play Sunderland at Roker Park in February 1987 must have wondered why Gates ran onto the field making gestures to the Press box that could only be interpreted in one way. The North East Press corps were bemused. Little did they know the reason. A message had been pinned on Gates' peg in the changing room reminding him of a card school dispute back in Ipswich some years before (nothing to be do with me, I hasten to add). Ian Atkins, a former Sunderland captain, had delivered the message when he went to the ground in the afternoon when the kit was being delivered and laid out for the match. It was signed by Ipswich journalist Dave Allard.

Ironically Gates is now a media man himself working on radio in the North East.

Brian Gayle
Defender, 1990 to 1991

Born: Kingston, 6 March 1965
Signed: 19 January 1990 from Manchester City
    for £330,000
Debut: *v.* Wolverhampton Wanderers (away),
    lost 1-2. 10 February 1990

Ipswich career:
61 starts (1 sub), 4 goals
Football League: 58, 4
FA Cup: (1)
Football League Cup: 3

Other clubs: Wimbledon, Manchester City,
    Sheffield United, Exeter City, Rotherham
    United, Bristol Rovers, Exeter City (again),
    Shrewsbury Town and Telford United.

Ipswich manager John Duncan was coming under pressure, mainly for his long-ball style of play, when he persuaded the Board to let him spend £330,000 on central defender Brian Gayle from Manchester City.

It turned out to be a terrific investment. Duncan departed and new boss John Lyall kept Gayle for a season before selling him to Sheffield United for £800,000. Dave Bassett had worked with Gayle at Wimbledon and wanted him as first-team captain at Bramall Lane. It was far too good an offer for Ipswich to turn down.

Brian Gayle (dark shirt, centre) in action against Port Vale at Portman Road. David Linighan is on the extreme left and Jason Dozzell appears to have won a heading duel with Robbie Earle on the right.

49

David Geddis
Centre forward, 1975 to 1979

Born: Carlisle, 12 March 1958
Signed: 19 August 1975 from apprentice
Debut: *v.* Derby County (away), drawn 0-0,
      14 May 1977

Ipswich career:
30 starts (26 subs), 6 goals
Football League: 26(17), 5
FA Cup: 2(1), 1
Football League Cup: (1)
UEFA Cup: (4)
European Cup Winners' Cup: 2(3)
Honours: England youth international

Other clubs: Luton (loan), Aston Villa, Luton
      (loan), Barnsley, Birmingham City, Brentford
      (loan), Shrewsbury Town, Swindon Town
      and Darlington.

David Geddis made only 30 starts for Ipswich Town, where he came through the youth ranks. The reason he appears in this book is because of his massive contribution in the 1978 FA Cup final success against Arsenal at Wembley. Bobby Robson picked him on the right wing for the first time in his career. There were special tactics devised for this one-off game. David's main task was to keep Gunners' left-back Sammy Nelson with his hands full. It turned out to be a cross from Geddis that led to the miskicked clearance by Willie Young that gave Roger Osborne his chance for glory with that 78th-minute winner. Robson was full of praise for Geddis, saying that it was perhaps the finest game of his career.

The following year, Geddis was fortunate to escape in a terrible car accident that claimed the life of another of Town's young players, Peter Canavan. It happened on the A12 between Colchester and Ipswich. Geddis was not to blame, but the memory of incident was just too much and he asked for a move to give him a change of environment. He was sold to Aston Villa for £300,000 – a good

price for a fringe player, even though he had won an FA Cup winner's medal.

Later in his career, he played in the lower divisions before taking up a coaching appointment at Middlesbrough under Bryan Robson. Changes the top at the Riverside Stadium meant another move, this time to Newcastle United, back to his old boss Bobby Robson.

Born: Seaham, 12 August 1962

Signed: 30 August 1985 from Seaham Red Star
for £3,000

Debut: v. Arsenal (away), lost 0-1, 19 October 1985

Ipswich career:

65 starts (17 subs), 13 goals

Football League: 54(12), 11

FA Cup: 3(1)

Football League Cup: 3(2)

Full Members' Cup: 5(2), 2

Other clubs: Manchester City, Birmingham City,
Stoke City, Burnley, Brentford and
Northampton Town.

Nigel Gleghorn was a Newcastle-on-Tyne fireman playing non-League football for Seaham Red Star when Bobby Ferguson signed him for £3,000 in August 1985. He was a left-sided midfield player – not particularly fast, but very difficult to dispossess. He fitted into Ferguson's pattern of play, but found it difficult to adapt to John Duncan's long-ball game that followed.

He wanted to leave when his contract expired and this was a glaring example of when a tribunal made a total nonsense of settling a transfer fee. The decision that Manchester City should pay only £47,500 for a midfield player with 11 goals in 66 games seemed a travesty. This was underlined by the fact that he later moved from Maine Road to Birmingham City for £170,000 in 1989 and later to Stoke City for £100,000 in October 1992.

Gleghorn was missed because he had been a far more effective player for Ipswich than his successor, Ian Redford, who had cost £200,000 from Dundee United. Bobby Ferguson had an entertaining turn of phrase and after one poor performance I heard that he said in the dressing room: 'I thought I'd bought a footballer, but all I've got is a fireman. Gleghorn, you sat on that wing like a big fat toad.' Gleghorn was a good footballer with his feet firmly on the ground. He also played Minor County cricket for Durham.

Nigel Gleghorn (right) races to congratulate Ian Atkins who had just scored a crucial goal against Oxford United in a First Division match in 1986.

Paul Goddard

Centre forward, 1991 to 1994

Born: Harlington (London), 12 October 1959
Signed: January 1991 from Millwall (free transfer)
Debut: *v.* Millwall (home), lost 0-3, 2 February 1991

Ipswich career:
74 starts (35 subs), 15 goals
Premiership: 22(21), 15
Football League: 37(6), 10
FA Cup: 6(8)
Football League Cup: 7
Full Members' Cup: 2
Honours: England cap v. Iceland at Reykjavik
  in 1982 (in which he scored), 8 under-21 caps

Other clubs: QPR, West Ham United, Derby
  County and Millwall.

Paul Goddard was a tremendously popular striker at QPR, West Ham, Newcastle United and Derby County. The welcome he received when he returned to Newcastle in an Ipswich shirt was superb. It compared to that given to Tony Mowbray on his first return to Middlesbrough.

Then Goddard moved to Millwall in 1989. Being a former Hammer, he was always fighting an uphill battle against prejudices at The Den. He moved around for big fees. West Ham paid £800,000, Newcastle £415,000, Derby County £415,000 and Millwall £800,000.

John Lyall rescued him from the Lions on a free transfer, but he arrived at Portman Road in February in the midst of a pretty dull season. There was little he could do to excite the locals, who had grown despondent. Only 8,937 turned up to watch Port Vale on the opening day of the following season. The fans had no inkling that it was to develop into the Second Division Championship-winning campaign of 1991/92. Goddard won the penalty against Vale that Neil Thompson converted for a 2-1 win.

Promotion was achieved and Goddard had the quality to hold his own in the Premiership. He was an excellent professional to have on the books. Known as 'Sarge' from his Boys' Brigade days, he and John Wark took control

of first-team affairs at the start of the 1994/95 season, with coach Mick McGiven handed another role within the club. Lyall was the overlord, but his resignation led to the appointment of George Burley that Christmas. Goddard, being perceived as a 'Lyall man', was asked to work with the all-important Youth Academy. Wark, who took less readily to coaching, did some scouting. In 2001/02, Goddard became assistant manager of West Ham United working with Glenn Roeder.

Bontcho Guentchev
Forward, 1992 to 1995

Born: Bulgaria, 7 July 1964
Signed: 11 December 1992 from Sporting Lisbon
Debut: *v.* Manchester City (home), won 3-1,
    12 December 1992

Ipswich career:
51 starts (24 subs), 11 goals
FA Premiership: 39(22), 6
FA Cup: 6(2), 5
Football League Cup: 6
Honours: Capped by Bulgaria 11 times

Other clubs: Lokomotiv, Etar, Sporting Lisbon,
    Luton Town, CSKA Sofia and Hendon Town.

The personable Bulgarian never had the qualifications to secure a work permit, but a letter signed by the president of the Bulgarian FA was enough to satisfy the bodies who mattered so he was able to join Ipswich Town from Bobby Robson's Sporting Lisbon. An impressive 12 caps and 6 goals looked a good strike rate at international level, until one discovered that he had played for Bulgaria in a friendly against Sweden in Gothenburg and the other appearances were 'A internationals' – whatever they meant.

Once in England he was allowed to stay, although regulations were later tightened up. He went on to play for Bulgaria in the World Cup in the United States in 1994 when they reached the semi-finals. He scored in a penalty shootout against Mexico in New York and appeared in the quarter-final victory over Germany and the semi-final defeat against Italy.

It was a red-letter day for Bontcho (how Town fans liked to chant his name) when he scored a hat-trick against Grimsby Town in the FA Cup in 1993. The first goal was a rising drive when the ball was played back by Jason Dozzell. The second was set up by Paul Goddard and the third in the 89th-minute was from a rebound after a shot from Claus Thomsen had bounced off the legs of goalkeeper Rhys Wilmot. After that match, Town director Harold Smith, with special duties to look after the media, appeared in the Press room saying in a voice loud enough for me to overhear: 'What a good hat-trick from Bontcho. He's the man Garnett tried to prevent us from signing.' I turned a deaf ear.

Guentchev departed to join Luton Town, but received a great reception from Ipswich fans when he appeared as substitute in a League match at Kenilworth Road at the end of March 1996. There would have been far less fuss over the Guentchev signing had Town manager John Lyall, when questioned over the player's caps, come clean and explained that he was trying to secure a quality player cheap. Instead, he threatened litigation if the story was printed – which virtually guaranteed its publication the very next day. I told Lyall I would think about it; I did for thirty seconds before discussing it with my editor and deciding to go ahead and print the facts. I felt sorry for Bontcho. It was not his fault.

Vlado Bozinoski, an Australian with a Macedonian background and an EU passport, was signed at the same time from Sporting Lisbon. He had command of several languages and was able to help Bontcho and his family to settle down in Suffolk.

Bryan Hamilton

Midfield, 1971 to 1975

Born: Belfast 31 December 1946
Signed: 12 August 1971 from Linfield for £18,000
Debut: v. Everton (home), drawn 0-0,
      14 August 1971

Ipswich career:
186 starts (13 subs), 56 goals
Football League: 142(11), 43
FA Cup: 11(1), 5
Football League Cup: 11(1), 3
Texaco Cup: 8, 2
UEFA Cup: 14, 3
Honours: 50 caps for Northern Ireland (21 while
      at Ipswich), 2 under-23 caps

Other clubs: (playing) Everton, Millwall, Swindon
      Town, Tranmere Rovers; (managing) Tranmere
      Rovers, Wigan Athletic, Leicester City, Wigan
      Athletic (again), Tranmere Rovers, Northern
      Ireland and Norwich City.

Quite a bargain from Linfield, Bryan Hamilton served Ipswich with distinction on the right side of midfield for more than four years. He had a strike rate during that time that few forwards could match.

It is a sore point with Bryan that he never played in an FA Cup final. It is almost unbelievable to think that he scored what seemed to be good goals in semi-final ties only for them to be ruled out by the same official. The man in question was referee Clive Thomas. In 1975, Ipswich fans will always remember the replay with West Ham at Stamford Bridge, the home of Chelsea. The linesman did not flag, the goal looked good enough, but Mr Thomas thought it was offside. It was 0-0 at the time but Ipswich were the better side and needed a breakthrough.

The 1977 semi-final was a Merseyside derby. It was the 89th minute of a classic tie when Hamilton had the winner in the net off his hip. Before the celebrations could begin, Mr Thomas had blown for an infringement. Maybe he thought Hamilton had handled the ball, but the

player has always insisted that was not the case. Hamilton commented: 'Referees should only give what they see, not what they think they see. Clive should have consulted the linesman. All he would say afterwards was that he disallowed it for an infringement. He would never say what that infringement was. It would be nice if he cleared it up one day.'

Hamilton, an automatic choice for Northern Ireland and more recently that country's coach, played 52 games for Everton before joining Millwall. He captained the London club in 1978 when Ipswich won 6-1 on their way to Wembley. The day will always be remembered for the hooliganism (comparable with that at Lazio a few years earlier). In an unguarded moment, an angry Bobby Robson said they should 'turn the flamethrowers' onto the hooligans. Of course he never expected to be quoted and had to backpedal considerably! One sympathised with his view, although only the less intelligent members of society took him literally.

Hamilton has been involved in management and coaching since he retired as a player. He has twice been called in to add his experience to George Burley's backroom staff at Portman Road. He also had a spell in charge of Norwich City.

Ken Hancock
Goalkeeper, 1964 to 1969

Born: Hanley, 25 November 1937
Signed: 12 December 1964 from Port Vale
Debut: *v.* Preston North End (away), lost 1-4,
    19 December 1964

Ipswich career:
180 starts
Football League: 163
FA Cup: 7
Football League Cup: 10

Other clubs: Port Vale, Tottenham Hotspur
    and Bury.

Bill McGarry needed to tighten up the defence. Roy Bailey was past his prime, Jim Thorburn played 14 successive matches (which was enough to suggest he would not be the long-term answer) and David Bevis was clearly third in the pecking order. McGarry looked to Port Vale, where he had started his playing career. Hancock had played 240 League matches in just over five years and had the credentials to be the steadying influence that was needed. He was an excellent signing at the time.

Hancock rather fancied himself as a rally driver. On one occasion he volunteered to provide me with some company in my car on the way home from a match in the North. I had a fairly quick GT Ford Cortina at the time and Ken was keen to get behind the wheel with his oversize driving gauntlets. He claimed to know a short-cut through Stoke-on-Trent, but my memory is of driving along cobbled back streets a shade too fast for my liking! My nerves were frayed and I was just hoping we could get back on the open road as quickly as possible.

Hancock was a highly rated goalkeeper. After David Best arrived at Portman Road, Hancock joined Tottenham Hotspur as cover for Pat Jennings and played three first-team games for the London club. He finished his career at Bury.

He always appeared to do the simple things without fuss. His sound positional sense meant that he did not need to fling himself around all that often. For a while he ran a country pub in the North but has now retired.

Thorburn had been signed from Raith Rovers by Jackie Milburn, having played in a relegated side and conceded a record number of 114 goals. At first Milburn laid the blame on the defence in front of him, but then signed Raith central defender Jack Bolton.

Thorburn cost £5,000 and thought it was a joke when he first heard of Town's interest. He had only been a part-timer in Scotland and had already qualified as a junior draughtsman.

Thorburn once admitted: 'When I look back on my time at Ipswich, I am sorry I didn't do better. I feel I let the club and the fans down.' On returning to Scotland, he played as a part-timer for St Mirren, who were then managed by Doug Millward.

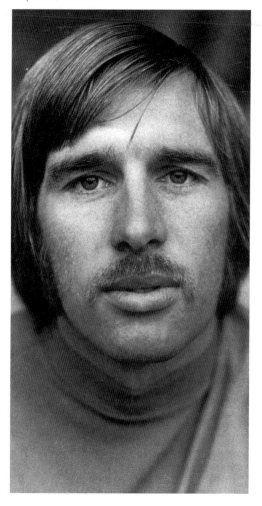

Born: Ipswich 25 July 1946
Signed: 22 July 1966 from juniors
Debut: *v.* Plymouth Argyle (away), lost 0-3,
    19 February 1966

Ipswich career:
171 starts (5 subs), 6 goals
Football League: 144(4), 6
FA Cup: 5, 1
Football League Cup: 8(1)
UEFA Cup: 6
Texaco Cup: 8

Other clubs: Grimsby Town, Cambridge United
    and Port Vale (manager 1977).

Colin Harper was a local lad who joined the youth scheme in Bill McGarry's time but did not become a regular first-team player until Bobby Robson took charge. He was ever-present at left-back in the League in the 1971/72 season, with Geoff Hammond and Mick Mills sharing the right-back spot.

A serious knee injury sustained in the Olympic Stadium in Rome in the UEFA Cup tie against Lazio in November 1973 tended to get overlooked in the furore that followed the match, when Lazio players and supporters went on the rampage. The Ipswich players stayed locked in the safety of the dressing room for a couple of hours until the worst of the trouble had died down. I joined them there after an extraordinary night that coincided with a strike by the National Union of Journalists. I tried to ring through my match report. The editor of the *East Anglian Daily Times*, Donald Simpson, answered the phone personally and told me that he required no report from me that night but would give me no explanation.

It was just as well as it turned out. Less than five minutes later, Italian fans, who had been burning British flags, had clambered over the seats into the Press box and kicked the phone from its socket. It was at that stage that I sought refuge with the players.

Lazio provided their official club coach to transport the Ipswich team away from the ground through the hostile crowd. Players were asked to draw the curtains and lie on the floor in case of broken windows. The hotel was still surrounded by angry Italians, so the party was taken to a restaurant in the hills outside Rome until the all-clear message was received. It was a massive story for Ipswich Town, which I was unable to report because of industrial action about which I knew nothing.

Harper played a few more games when his knee recovered, but ended his career as manager of Port Vale in succession to Roy Sproson. Then he returned to Ipswich where he became a builder. He has creative ideas on how to improve executive boxes at football grounds and Tottenham Hotspur have become one of his clients.

Danny Hegan

Inside forward, 1963 to 1969

Born: Coatbridge 14 June 1943
Signed: 29 July 1963 from Sunderland for £10,000
Debut: *v.* Bolton Wanderers (away), lost 0-6,
18 September 1963

Ipswich career:
230 starts, 38 goals
Football League: 207, 34
FA Cup: 11, 3
Football League Cup: 12, 1
Honours: 7 caps for Northern Ireland after
leaving Ipswich

Other clubs: Albion Rovers, Sunderland, West
Bromwich Albion and Wolves.

Jackie Milburn proved to be an excellent judge of talent in attacking players. It's a pity his man management was not so good, because he expected high standards of professionalism off the field that did not come naturally to all the players under his control. He was too lenient as a manager, the exact opposite of his successor Bill McGarry. Danny Hegan was a brilliant footballer recruited from Sunderland. He soon thrived and established himself as the midfield general during McGarry's strict time in charge.

In fact, McGarry was so impressed that a £45,000 offer for Hegan was his first move in the transfer market after succeeding Ronnie Allen as manager of Wolves. The snag was that McGarry had valued Hegan at £80,000 a few weeks earlier while still at Portman Road. Needless to say, the bid was laughed out of court by the Ipswich directors.

Although Bill Baxter was the regular captain during this period, Hegan deputised on four different occasions. He missed only one match, the East Anglian derby at Norwich in 1967/68, when Ipswich were champions of the Second Division.

Although Town were back at the top level and Bobby Robson had taken over at the helm, Hegan was unsettled by Wolves' interest and wanted to get away. In May 1969 he moved to West Bromwich in a deal that brought Ian Collard (valued at £60,000) and a £30,000 cheque to Ipswich.

Hegan played in one match that cost me a sizeable bet. Ipswich had drawn 0-0 at Southport in the third round of the FA Cup at Haig Avenue. I had seen the match and was not particularly impressed by the side managed by Billy Bingham. Bob Crisp, the *East Anglian Daily Times* leader writer and former South African Test cricketer, asked what odds I would give him on a Southport win. I said 4-1 and was amazed when he wanted £10 on them. Suffice to say that Southport won 3-2 at Portman Road and to this day I cannot understand why McGarry played Ken Thompson, an inexperienced local-born half-back, up front that night. Mr Crisp, father of one-time Colchester United chairman Jonathan, was more than happy to take my money. Paying him £40 made quite a dent in the bank balance of a young reporter earning less than a tenner a week.

Hegan eventually linked up with McGarry again at Wolves in 1970 and played in the 1972 UEFA Cup final against Tottenham, which the Londoners won. His departure from Portman Road made space for the development of a skilful young South African called Colin Viljoen. After his football days were over, he coached at holiday camps.

Mick Hill was certainly a strange lad but he was not short of talent. He was Ipswich Town's leading scorer in the 1971/72 season when he had a spell of six goals in six games. He started as a Cardiff City junior, but was released and took a clerical job in Hereford. His father persuaded him to try again and he impressed with non-League team Bethesda Athletic before joining Sheffield United in September 1965 and scoring on his debut.

Bobby Robson paid £33,000 for him in October 1969 and he netted a memorable solo goal against Liverpool, televised on *Match of the Day*. For some reason, Mick became disillusioned with football and lived in a caravan near Chantry Park, where he

Born: Hereford, 3 December 1947
Signed: 17 October 1969 from Sheffield United for £30,000
Debut: *v.* Arsenal (away), draw 0-0, 25 October 1969

Ipswich career:
74 starts (3 subs), 20 goals
Football League: 63(3), 18
FA Cup: 9, 2
Football League Cup: 2
Honours: 2 full caps for Wales

Other clubs: Cardiff City, Sheffield United, Crystal Palace and Cape Town City.

Mick Hill in a battle for the ball with barrel-chested Scottish international Dave Mackay in a match against Tottenham Hotspur.

was happy to feed the ducks and coach kids in the park. Then he made a comeback in November 1972 as substitute in a 2-2 draw at home to Leeds. This attracted the attention of Malcolm Allison, who was then in charge at Crystal Palace. I remember Robson calling me to say that Palace were prepared to pay £35,000 and Mick was setting off for London by train. I asked if anyone was going with him just to make sure he arrived. Mick might easily have had a change of heart and got out at Chelmsford! Robson saw the point.

Mick later emigrated to South Africa and scored for Cape Town City in their 1976/77 South African Cup final. Mick should not be confused with midfielder David Hill, who was signed by John Duncan from Scunthorpe for £90,000 in July 1988. The second Ipswich Hill broke his leg in a Combination match against Norwich and, after making 61 Second Division appearances, returned to Scunthorpe for £30,000 in September 1991. He spent two years at Lincoln and then played for a while in Ireland.

Matt Holland

Midfield, joined 1997

Matt Holland established himself as a household name when he starred for the Republic of Ireland in the 2002 World Cup finals in Japan and South Korea. A great 52nd minute equaliser against Cameroon with a thirty-yard right-foot strike in Niigata made him something of a hero.

He was inches wide with what was almost a carbon copy after twenty-five minutes of the match against Germany at Ibarakii. Hitting the crossbar in the penalty shoot-out with Spain with a quarter-final place there for the taking was bitterly disappointing. He was not the only member of the Irish side unable to beat Spanish goalkeeper, Iker Casillas. David Connolly and Kevin Kilbane both had shots saved.

Eligible for selection through his grandmother, Matt is a Lancashire lad from Bury. He broke into Mick McCarthy's squad as a mere fringe member. He made a low-key international debut in a 1-1 draw against Macedonia in Skopje in October 1999.

Everyone started to take notice when he scored a cracking 72nd minute equaliser in Portugal to enable the Irish to come away with

Born: Bury (Lancs), 11 April 1974
Signed: 5 August 1997
Debut: *v*. QPR (away), draw 0-0, 9 August 1997

Ipswich career:
259 starts (1 subs), 39 goals
Premiership: 76, 6
Football League: 138, 25
Play-offs: 7, 2
FA Cup: 10
Football League Cup: 22(1), 6
UEFA Cup: 6
Honours: Republic of Ireland international,
      19 caps as of the end of 2002 World Cup

Other clubs: West Ham United and Bournemouth.

a 1-1 draw. Injury to Charlton's Mark Kinsella meant that Holland became first choice alongside the dominating but rebellious Roy Keane in the later World Cup build-up matches.

When Roy Keane left the Irish squad in the Far East before a ball had been kicked in anger, Holland was presented with the opportunity to grow in stature. He took on his extra responsibilities in brilliant fashion.

He helped the Irish to reach the last sixteen. It was not only on the field that he proved influential. He was excellent at handling the media and showed full support for McCarthy in the difficult days after the unrepentant Roy Keane returned to Ireland.

Holland joined West Ham as a teenager after he was rejected by Arsenal for being too small. Finding it hard to make an early breakthrough at Upton Park, he lowered his sights and joined Bournemouth on a free transfer in January 1995.

His leadership qualitites soon became obvious. He was appointed team captain of a cash-strapped club. He scored 18 goals in a total of 104 appearances for the Cherries. He also turned out twice against Ipswich in the two-leg Worthington Cup tie in the autumn of 1996. Many fans missed the start of the second leg at Dean Court due to traffic chaos on the M25.

Matt's potential was spotted by Town boss George Burley and he arrived at Portman Road

in 1997. He immediately became an automatic choice in central midfield.

Up to the start of the 2002/03 season, he had not missed the start of any Premiership, Football League, play-off or UEFA Cup match the club had played. He was disappointed when only on the bench for a Football League Cup tie at Millwall in the 2000/01 season, but at least he played in the second half. Then he was left out altogether in a Football League Cup tie at Crewe, just to give him a break from a heavy League season. He also watched the FA Cup third round tie at Dagenham & Redbridge from the stand, when it was felt that other squad members could achieve the result required.

It's been a wonderful period in his career during which his disciplinary record has been simply amazing. The only foul to land him in a spot of minor bother was at Sunderland in 1998 when he flew into an uncharacteristic lunge at Alex Rae. He has never experienced a red card nor suffered a suspension.

The Ipswich supporters voted him their Player of the Year in 1998. He succeeded Tony Mowbray as first-team captain at the start of the 1999/2000 season and achieved his dream of lifting a trophy at Wembley when Ipswich beat Barnsley in the Division One play-off the following May.

He can be compared with a former Ipswich midfield dynamo, Brian Talbot, for his sheer hard work. He runs from box to box and picks up his share of goals in much the same manner as John Wark but, of course, is not so prolific.

He can also crack a powerful free-kick. In February 2002, Everton goalkeeper Steve Simonsen was picking the ball out of the net at Goodison Park after Holland had struck the ball venomously with his right foot from twenty-five yards.

Holland's World Cup exploits have enhanced his reputation as a player. His weekly articles in the *Sunday Independent* and the cool manner with which he handles Press conferences suggest that, when his playing days are over, there could well be a niche for him in the media. He is a great ambassador for football.

Tony Humes

Defender, 1983 to 1992

As a twenty-one-year-old, the lad from Blyth played for Town in five different positions, including centre forward. He was generally regarded as a resolute defender who had nine-and-a-half years at Portman Road, during which he suffered far more than his fair share of injuries.

Two broken arms, a broken jaw, a broken foot, a cartilage operation and a hernia operation all kept him out of the side for lengthy periods. He broke his jaw in a clash of heads with Frank Stapleton at Blackburn. Stitches were needed inside the jaw, which was wired. He could only eat through a straw.

He was signed by Ipswich when he left school after being spotted by scout John Carruthers. He progressed through the apprentice ranks conveyor belt at the same time as Mark Brennan and Jon Hallworth.

He scored his first League goals in a 3-2 defeat at Leeds. The first was from a rebound from a shot by Ian Cranson. The second was a splendid header from a corner. His best goal came in the televised FA Cup tie against Manchester United in January 1988, when he found the net with a spectacular header.

Born: Blyth, 19 March 1966
Signed: 26 May 1983 from apprentice
Debut: *v.* Blackburn Rovers (away), drawn 0-0, 29 November 1986

Ipswich career:
127 starts (13 subs), 12 goals
Football League: 107(13), 10
Play-offs: 2
FA Cup: 4, 1
Football League Cup: 6
Full Members' Cup: 8, 1

Other club: Wrexham

He moved to Wrexham in March 1992 for £40,000, when it became clear that he did not feature in John Lyall's plans at Portman Road. He played his part in the FA Cup upset against Ipswich at the Racecourse Ground when Wrexham won 2-1 after Adam Tanner had conceded a penalty in the 88th minute – Adrian Paz and Phil Whelan both hit the bar for Ipswich late on. His defensive partner for Wrexham that day was Barry Hunter, nephew of Town's Allan.

Tony Humes is on the far right of the picture in the days when the stands at Portman Road were far from full.

Born: Sion Mills (NI), 30 June 1946
Signed: 9 September 1971 from Blackburn R.
Debut: *v.* Leicester City (home), lost 1-2,
   11 September 1971

Ipswich career:
354 starts, one as substitute, 10 goals
Football League: 280, 8 goals
FA Cup: 26
Football League Cup: 17, 2
UEFA Cup: 21
European Cup Winners' Cup: 2(1)
Texaco Cup: 8
Honours: 53 full caps for Northern Ireland (47
   while at Ipswich). 1 Northern Ireland
   under-23 cap; captained his country

Other clubs: Coleraine, Oldham Athletic,
   Blackburn Rovers and Colchester United.

'Big Al' became the most popular central defender ever to turn out for the Town. The highlight of his eleven-year spell at Portman Road was winning the FA Cup final against Arsenal at Wembley in 1978. The low point was probably the moment he missed the penalty in the shoot-out in Leipzig that ended the club's UEFA Cup run in 1974. It was such a cruel blow because Hunter had been a rock at the heart of the Ipswich defence that night after Mick Mills had been sent off.

Firstly there was the partnership of Hunter and Derek Jefferson, the short-sighted but wholehearted central defender, who had trouble timing his tackles under the floodlights. This was followed by the legendary pairing of Hunter and Kevin Beattie. They were nicknamed 'Bacon and Eggs' by Bobby Robson. Both players liked smoking and seemed none the worse for it at the time.

A knee injury (from which a pint of fluid had been drained off) had made Hunter doubtful for the FA Cup final. It was arranged that he should undergo an 11 a.m. fitness test on the morning of the match. Hunter, desperate to play, could not wait. He was on the lawn of the Sopwell House Hotel, giving himself a private test. Other players had got wind of it and were urging him on him from their bedrooom windows. There was a tremendous cheer when he gave them the

thumbs up. He underwent surgery, as did Beattie, after the season was over.

Born at Sion Mills, not too far from the Bushmills Distillery, Hunter started his career with Coleraine. His first club in England was Oldham Athletic. Then he moved on to Blackburn Rovers. Ipswich signed him for £60,000 in a deal that saw Bobby Bell move in the opposite direction. It proved to be an inspired signing, with all credit to scout Ron Gray – who was never in doubt about the Irishman's quality, even though Hunter had an off day when being watched for the first time by Robson. He had previously caught the eye in the home internationals and attracted the interest of Leeds and Everton. Hunter was seldom predictable. When invited to display his skills to Everton in a practice match arranged especially for him, he didn't fancy joining the Merseyside club. He said that he had a groin strain and watched the practice from the grandstand.

One of Hunter's greatest games was in the fourth of those FA Cup quarter-final battles with Leeds United on the neutral Leicester City ground. Beattie dropped out through injury and seventeen-year-old John Wark was introduced for his first taste of senior football against just about the most powerful team in the land. Hunter guided Wark through the minefield.

Hunter became player-manager of Colchester United, but did not really enjoy the lifestyle. He then took a job on Felixstowe docks, which he gave up when invited to work as coach at Layer Road with Mike Walker. Walker lost his job with the U's on a high. Hunter then had a spell out of football when he did commendable work teaching carpentry at the Belstead Special School. More recently he has been operating as a scout working for his old boss, Bobby Robson, at Newcastle.

Born: Morpeth, 5 September 1948
Signed: February 1966 from apprentice
Debut: *v.* Shrewsbury Town, FA Cup third round
(home), won 4-1, 28 January 1967

Ipswich career:
172 starts (3 subs), 1 goal
Football League 163(3), 1
FA Cup: 6
Football League Cup: 3

Other clubs: Wolverhampton Wanderers,
Sheffield Wednesday and Hereford United.

He was Bill McGarry's type of no-nonsense defender. Bobby Robson said: 'He tackled like Nobby Stiles and was short-sighted like him.' Certainly Derek had problems with the glare of the floodlights, which accounted for many of his mistimed challenges. I first discovered just how short-sighted he was when playing tennis on the hard court at home with Derek, Mick Mills and Joe Broadfoot. Derek seldom picked up the volleys at the net.

A likeable lad, he could get a bit excitable after a drink or two. He was, however, not the sort of person you would have expected to become deeply involved in religion. Once a solid defender, he is now a powerful and confident orator on religious topics.

On Boxing Day 1968 he was very late with a challenge on Peter Osgood of Chelsea and became the first Ipswich player to be sent off in a senior match at Portman Road. Town fans nicknamed him 'Chopper' and he began to

believe his own publicity. He felt he was in the same exclusive hard men's club as Norman Hunter (Leeds), Tommy Smith (Liverpool) and Ron Harris (Chelsea).

Jefferson was Ipswich Town's captain for seven matches when Mick Mills was injured. He and fellow central defender Bobby Bell were once described as 'animals' by Jimmy Hill on television.

Sadly, Jefferson's first marriage went off the rails. He blamed himself for ninety-five per cent of the problems. It was while he was with Wolves that he became involved in heavy drinking (champagne rather than spirits). He had been known to stay up all night drinking and then go straight to training.

Jefferson spent two close seasons in the States when he played against the legendary Pele. He had two years as player-coach at Hereford and then went to the States again. By the time he returned in 1978, his marriage had broken up.

On a visit to his parents at Bedlington, he accompanied his mother to a Baptist chapel. That visit changed his life. A young man at the front stood up and told how he had discovered someone who loved him a great deal, Jesus Christ. Jefferson broke down in tears.

After a few years as coach at Birmingham City under Jim Smith, he decided to quit professional football. He met his new wife, Linda, daughter of a Pentecostal preacher, on a Christian holiday. Then he gave up his well-paid job as a sales rep for Glaxo to devote himself full-time to the Church.

David 'Jonty' Johnson
Centre forward, 1972 to 1976

Born: Liverpool, 23 October 1951
Signed: 30 October 1972 from Everton
Debut: v. Leeds United (home), drawn 2-2,
    4 November 1972

Ipswich career:
174 starts (4 subs), 46 goals
Football League: 134(3), 35
FA Cup: 15, 4
Football League Cup: 8, 5
UEFA Cup: 13(1), 2
Texaco Cup: 8
Honours: 8 full caps for England (3 with Ipswich)
    and 9 under-23 caps

Other clubs: Everton, Liverpool, Everton (again),
    Barnsley, Manchester City, Preston North
    End and Tulsa (USA).

David Johnson's arrival at Portman Road saw Town's leading scorer Rod Belfitt move in the opposite direction. Some fans thought Bobby Robson had taken leave of his senses, but little did they know. Johnson's speed and bravery, alongside Trevor Whymark's awesome heading ability, made them a formidable force that played a large part in putting Ipswich on the European stage.

Ipswich had drawn 2-2 at Everton, whose manager, Harry Catterick, expressed an interest in Belfitt. This gave Robson his chance to suggest a deal involving Johnson, whom he had been watching for some time. Belfitt had cost £55,000 from Leeds. He agreed to join Everton with Ipswich happy to pay an extra £40,000.

A Liverpool lad, 'Jonty' as he was called, took a nasty boot in the testicles in the home leg of the UEFA Cup tie against Lazio in 1973. Stitches were needed in the most delicate parts. The following week, Town chairman John Cobbold and a fellow director asked how the injury was progressing. Johnson unzipped his trousers and said: 'Have a look for yourselves' as he slapped the injured part on the boardroom table.

Johnson broke into the England team but was transferred to Liverpool for £200,000 in 1976, which made way for the arrival of Paul Mariner – who also became an England star. During his six years at Anfield, he picked up four Championship medals, three European Cup medals and three League Cup medals. No wonder he says: 'Given the chance, I would choose exactly the same career all over again. I can look back and say that I was more than a First Division player. I have medals to keep and I played for the best team in Europe.' He eventually lost his place to goalscoring sensation Ian Rush at Anfield.

Johnson scored on his England debut against Wales and three days later found the net against Scotland. In 1980, he made five international appearances and scored two of England's trio in a 3-1 win over Argentina.

I sold him the premises in Tacket Street where he set up a high-class clothes shop called 'Jonty'. It had previously been the Rainbow Grill, but I decided that the restaurant business was not for me (in addition to journalism) when I discovered trout in the deep freeze when it was not on the menu. My stock controller – perhaps too concerned with not burning an omelette – thought she had ordered sprouts but obviously never checked the delivery. 'Jonty' is still trading, but David has not been involved for many years.

Since his retirement, he has been a financial adviser to a Liverpool-based insurance firm. He also does media work and after-dinner speaking.

David Johnson

Centre forward, 1997 to 2000

David was signed from Bury for £1.1 million at a time when Ipswich needed a boost in attack, having missed out on signing Kevin Phillips from Watford in the previous close season. He was the second striker of that name to lead the Ipswich front line with distinction, although he could hardly claim to be in the same class as England international 'Jonty' of the 1970s.

He helped Manchester United lift the FA Youth Cup in 1995 and won England schoolboy honours. Sir Alex Ferguson let him go on a free transfer, which proved a godsend for hard-up Bury.

Only 5ft 6ins, he was very quick and scored in an impressive debut against Wolves at Molineux in November 1997. He was also brought down for a penalty in that match (which Adam Tanner missed). He became such a prolific scorer in Division One that he earned a call-up for the England under-21 squad to face the Greeks in Norwich. He was on the bench but did not appear, which meant that he was able to keep his international options open.

He played friendly matches for Jamaica and England B, but rejected the opportunity to turn out for Wales. There was also talk of selection for Scotland. He was Town's top scorer with 22 Division One goals in the promotion season, but he never seemed on the same wavelength as new signing Marcus Stewart. In the play-offs, it was only when Johnson went off injured that Stewart blossomed and Ipswich were successful. This was the pattern in the semi-final at Bolton and in the final against Barnsley at Wembley.

He was too often outspoken. He became involved in a momentary bust-up on the field with Jim Magilton in a match at West Bromwich. This was caught by the television cameras when most people in the Press box at the Hawthorns had not even seen it. It transpired that Johnson and Magilton had become next-door neighbours. This led to a newspaper backpage heading claiming they were 'neighbours from hell'. It seemed a bit harsh.

A wonder save by Fabien Barthez prevented him from getting off the mark with a header in the Premiership against Manchester United. Confidence drained away and he was sold to

Born: Jamaica, 15 August 1976

Signed: 30 November 1997 from Bury for £1.1 million (Chris Swailes as £300,000 makeweight)

Debut: *v.* Wolverhampton Wanderers (away), drawn 1-1, 15 November 1997

Ipswich career:
147 starts (10 subs), 62 goals
Premiership: 6(8)
Football League: 115(2), 55
Play-offs: 7
FA Cup: 7, 2
Football League Cup: 12, 5
Honours: Jamaican international, England B international

Other clubs: Manchester United, Bury, Nottingham Forest and Burnley.

Nottingham Forest for £3 million. This was George Burley's best piece of business so far as selling was concerned.

David Johnson fires past Port Vale goalkeeper Kevin Pilkington at Portman Road in April 2000. Ipswich won the match 2-0.

Chris Kiwomya

Forward, 1988 to 1995

Born: Bradford, 2 December 1969
Signed: 31 March 1987 from apprentice
Debut: *v.* Bradford City (home), drawn 1-1,
    24 September 1988

Ipswich career:
230 starts (29 subs), 62 goals
Premiership: 85(5), 18
Football League: 112(23), 33
FA Cup: 14, 2
Football League Cup: 14(1), 8
Full Members' Cup: 5, 1

Other clubs: Arsenal, Le Havre and QPR.

Slightly built, with a terrific turn of foot, he was nicknamed 'Benson' when he arrived as a junior because he looked so much like the American television comedy star. John Lyall changed that to 'Lino' because he was always on the floor.

He was Town's leading scorer in the inaugural year of the Premiership. Ten of his goals came in the League and the other half-dozen in the League Cup, including a first-half hat-trick against Wigan Athletic. The previous year he had played a leading role in the team that was promoted from the Second Division. He formed a good understanding with Paul Goddard. The Kiwomya family comes from Bradford. His elder brother, Andy, was a professional with Barnsley, Sheffield Wednesday and Bradford City. His mother was an athlete – which perhaps accounts for his pace.

Unlucky to miss out on an England under-21 cap, he was an unused substitute against Germany and then tore a thigh muscle which ruled him out of playing against Turkey when it seemed that his chance must come. Kiwomya used to train with Leeds United when a pupil at St Bede's School. He was spotted by Town scout Terry Rhodes and was another of those home-produced stars who had to be sold eventually to keep the bank manager happy.

He became the last player to be signed for Arsenal by George Graham. With a new management team in place at Highbury, he found it hard to establish himself and had spells on loan at Le Havre and in Selangor.

Mick Lambert

Winger, 1967 to 1979

Born: Balsham (Cambs), 20 May 1950
Signed: 11 December 1967 from apprentice
Debut: v. Coventry City (home), drawn 0-0,
    25 March 1969

Ipswich career:
219 starts (44 subs), 45 goals
Football League: 180(30), 39
FA Cup: 16(5), 3
Football League Cup: 12(5), 2
UEFA Cup: 3(4)
Texaco Cup: 8, 1

Other club: Peterborough United.

I first met Mick Lambert when Bill McGarry introduced him to my Saxmundham cricket team during a long weekend tour of Bournemouth organised by Reg Tyrrell, my club umpire and Ipswich Town's chief scout. McGarry was never prepared to bat until Tyrrell was there in the white coat. On one occasion at HMS *Ganges*, I was fielding as a substitute fielder at square leg next to Tyrrell. McGarry was run out by a couple of feet but Tyrrell turned to me and asked: 'Do I dare give the boss out?' Thankfully the finger went up. Lambert was an excellent cricketer, who had been on the ground staff at Lord's and fielded in a Test match against the West Indies. It was certainly a unique double

when he also came on as substitute in the FA Cup final after Roger Osborne had gone off in a daze after scoring what turned out to be the winner against Arsenal.

A brave, direct winger who liked to shoot, Lambert was well established in the side when he had a clash of heads with Chelsea's Gary Locke in February 1974. He went to hospital with a fractured skull.

Lambert played in one of Town's greatest games, the 0-0 draw with Real Madrid in the Bernabeu Stadium. Bobby Robson's tactics of attacking from the outset took the Spanish club by surprise. Ipswich won on aggregate, but they also did more than enough to deserve victory on the night and stunned the Spaniards.

Lambert moved to Peterborough, where Peter Morris was manager. Morris rang me for a fitness report on Lambert before he made the signing. He was back in full training after injury at that time, but the daily drive from Capel St Mary to Peterborough took its toll. Later a call from Morris suggested that he was more than a little disappointed.

Lambert was also a very handy tennis player and has also taken up bowls.

Cyril Lea

Half-back, 1964 to 1969

Born: Moss (near Wrexham), 5 August 1934
Signed: 17 November 1964 from Leyton Orient
Debut: v. Charlton Athletic (home), drew 1-1,
    21 November 1964

Ipswich career:
119 starts (4 subs), 2 goals
Football League: 103(4), 2 goals
FA Cup: 8
Football League Cup: 8
Representative honours: 2 full caps for Wales

Other club: Leyton Orient.

How long Cyril Lea would have stayed on the field before being shown a red card in today's environment is a moot point – although, of course, I feel sure he would have adapted very quickly. The red-haired Welsh midfielder took no prisoners and played very much in the style of his manager, Bill McGarry. It was just the approach Ipswich needed at the time to consolidate. Relegation from the First Division was followed by early-season weeks spent under a real threat of a further demotion. Lea was signed from Leyton Orient and became the fourth Ipswich Town captain that season, the others being Bill Baxter, John Elsworthy and Mick McNeil.

In 1965 he won he was called up by Wales. He was involved in a 5-0 victory over Northern Ireland in Belfast on his debut. Then he played in a 4-1 defeat at the hands of Italy in Florence. Lea was immensely popular with Ipswich supporters and, when Bill McGarry decided to take on the challenge of Wolverhampton Wanderers in succession to Ronnie Allen in November 1968, it was Lea who was named as caretaker-manager. This was because Sammy Chung, the first-team coach, decided to follow McGarry.

When Bobby Robson was appointed, it was one of the conditions laid down by the board that Lea should stay. They worked in harmony until the summer of 1979, the year after Town's FA Cup success over Arsenal, when he left to take up an appointment as coach at Stoke City.

While at Ipswich there was a match at Nottingham Forest that was called off at lunchtime because of frost in the shadow of one of the stands. Bobby Robson asked me if I could give him and Cyril a lift to London to watch a match as the players preferred to return home on the coach.

I warned them that my Datsun Estate, although it had done less than 10,000 miles, had been torn apart by a greyhound. The lining of the roof was hanging down in drapes and the springs were emerging through the passenger's seat. Furthermore, the greyhound in question was in the back, which had been filled with straw. Robson and Lea, left with no other options, agreed. Robson pulled rank and chose the front seat, leaving Lea in the straw with the hound.

Little did Robson know that the greyhound always jumped into the front when the car was in motion and curled up in front of the passenger's seat with his head on the gearbox. I recall that we saw Arsenal reserves at Highbury that afternoon and arrived just in time for kick-off.

Lea stayed in football after retiring as a player. He worked for the Welsh FA together with Mike Smith. The same partnership had a spell in charge of Hull City between 1979 and 1982. Lea was manager of Colchester United between 1983 and 1986, before Mike Walker took over. In the past decade he has been youth coach at West Bromwich, has scouted for George Burley at Ipswich and has more recently worked with the youth squad at Rushden & Diamonds, where former Ipswich player Brian Talbot is manager.

Cyril Lea (in foreground) with fellow coach Roy McCrohan, a former Norwich City player.

Born: Edinburgh, 15 July 1955
Signed: 15 June 1955 from Brighton & Hove Albion
Debut: *v.* Bournemouth (home), won 1-0,
    8 October 1955

Ipswich career:
375 starts, 49 goals
Football League: 344, 43
FA Cup: 19, 4
Football League Cup: 8, 1
European Cup: 1, 0
FA Charity Shield: 1, 1
Other matches: 2, 0

Other clubs: Chelsea and Brighton & Hove Albion.

Jimmy Leadbetter was the thinking footballer Alf Ramsey needed down the left to make his deep-lying winger tactics effective. He went to school within seven-iron range of the Heart of Midlothian ground at Tynecastle. There was football in the family because his father had played for Bathgate, a club long-since out of the League. Nicknamed 'Sticks' by Town fans, Jimmy never really looked like a professional footballer. The wrinkles round his eyes made him look too old for a start. Looks can be deceptive, however, as many opponents discovered.

Jimmy came to Ipswich as an inside forward but soon took the number eleven shirt from George McLuckie and kept the job season after season as he collected championship medals for the Third Division (South), the Second Division and the First.

He played as an amateur for Murrayfield Athletic when he was seventeen years old. Then came National Service – an enforced break from civilian life that the youngsters of today will not fully understand. He was stationed in the Royal Artillery in Dover and then in Gibraltar, where he played under Johnny Wheeler (ex-Tranmere, Bolton and Liverpool) in the Combined Services side.

On his return to Scotland he joined Edinburgh Thistle, a nursery club for Hibernian. He won a Scottish Juvenile Cup medal with Thistle before turning professional with Ammandale.

In 1949, Billy Birrell, the Chelsea manager, spotted his talent. He spent three seasons at Stamford Bridge, during which he managed only three senior appearances. He was the first player to leave when Ted Drake became manager, moving to Brighton in an exchange deal involving Johnny McNichol. He had more joy down in Sussex, being a regular in the first team under Billy Lane.

He had played 120 first-team games when he asked for a transfer. He was never officially placed on the list, but moved to Ipswich nonetheless in 1955 and never looked back.

Leadbetter became a vital cog in Ramsey's slick machine. He had very little pace but possessed an uncanny vision and developed a perfect understanding with Ted Phillips and

Ray Crawford. Timing the release of the ball was crucial for Ted's thunderbolt long shots and Ray's lethal finishing at close quarters. He was allowed to play to his strengths, which meant that he was able to achieve a great deal more at Ipswich under Ramsey than he might have expected to do with any other club at that time.

On leaving Ipswich, he joined Sudbury Town and stayed in East Anglia for a while before a return to his native Scotland, where he took a job as a driver delivering newspapers. He has always kept in touch with Portman Road through Miss Pat Godbold – who does such a splendid job liaising with former players.

Born: Hartlepool, 9 January 1965
Signed: 23 June 1988 from Shrewsbury Town for
    £300,000
Debut: *v.* Stoke City (away), drawn 1-1,
    27 August 1988

Ipswich career:
325 starts (3 sub), 13 goals
Premiership: 111(1), 4
Football League: 164(1), 8
FA Cup: 18, 1
Football League Cup: 21(1)
Anglo-Italian Cup: 1
Full Members' Cup: 10

Other clubs: Hartlepool United, Derby County,
    Shrewsbury Town, Blackpool, Dunfermline
    and Southport.

David Linighan, the younger brother of Andy who played for Norwich and Arsenal among other, was signed by John Duncan for £300,000 from Shrewsbury Town. He was secured to bolster a defence that had lost Ian Atkins (to Birmingham) and Ian Cranson (to Sheffield Wednesday) the previous March. He is a member of a famous Hartlepool footballing family.

Linighan's star had been waning in the final months of Duncan's reign as manager, but the arrival of John Lyall saw him promoted to be first-team captain. He responded well becoming Player of the Year in 1990/91, when he settled down alongside Brian Gayle.

Linighan was in the Ipswich side, going well for promotion at the time, that slumped to a 5-0 defeat at Port Vale on New Year's Day in 1990. The setback ended an eleven-match unbeaten run in the League, but the second half of the season was a massive disappointment (although the team proved they could rise to the big occasion with a notable FA Cup victory over Leeds United at Elland Road).

Linighan owned a Staffordshire bull terrier which was well known in Hadleigh, where he lived. One day Dave Allard, the football writer for the *Evening Star*, agreed to take Linighan's car to a match up North. When he agreed he had no idea that the dog was to be a passenger. Peter Trevivian, the Ipswich first-team coach at the time, was delegated to travel with Allard to keep an eye on the animal.

John Wark was sharing a hotel room with Linighan the night before the match. Linny had chosen the bed nearest to the bathroom. The Staffie was at the foot of Linighan's bed.

All was well until Wark needed to visit the bathroom in the night. Linighan was fast asleep, but the dog growled whenever Wark made a move to get out of bed. The braver Wark became, the louder the dog growled. It was clearly no time for taking chances. There was nothing for it but to wake Linighan up to keep his dog under control.

There was a well-publicised incident when Linighan did not appear for the second half of a match at Portman Road. Town coach Mick McGiven said his central defender had been ruled out by an injury. Speaking to players in Alan Brazil's Black Adder pub on Saturday night, it was apparent that there had been a row. I drew the short straw to phone McGiven on the Sunday morning to give him the chance to revise his story in the light of what was now known. He would not do this. Indeed, he objected to this intrusion to his home life. There was a climb-down from the club later in the week. McGiven's post-match Press conferences were always a bit of fun because there were wagers going among journalists as to how many times he would say 'in fairness'. You tried to keep the conference going until your number approached.

Linighan joined Blackpool for £90,000 in January 1996. Then he had a spell in Scotland with Dunfermline before turning out for Blackpool. When staying at Paul Mason's excellent guest house in Southport he said that Linny was 'on the tools'. When translated that meant that he was working as a carpenter.

David Linighan in typical defensive action winning a high ball in a match at Portman Road. Romeo Zondervan is seen in the background.

David became top scorer with 18 goals in his first season at Portman Road after John Duncan signed him from Wigan Athletic for £80,000 in June 1987. He applied himself with great enthusiasm and was sharp enough to win a couple of England under-21 caps in 1988.

Support for Ipswich, especially at home, was becoming tepid. Lowe once said, not for publication at the time: 'The 3,000 fans at Wigan make more noise than the cardboard cut-outs at Ipswich'.

He coached Needham Market and was then sold to Leicester City for £250,000 – a healthy profit. He had a League career in which he scored 133 goals in 562 games. He rejoined Wigan for £125,000 in March 1996 when John Deehan was manager. When he hung his boots up he became a regional FA coach.

Born: Liverpool, 30 August 1965
Signed: 26 June 1987 from Wigan Athletic for £80,000
Debut: v. Aston Villa (home), drawn 1-1, 15 August 1987

Ipswich career:
144 starts (15 subs), 42 goals
Football League: 121(13), 37
FA Cup: 3
Football League Cup: 10, 2
Full Members' Cup: 10(2), 3
Honours: England under-21 and youth caps

Other clubs: Wigan Athletic, Port Vale, Leicester City, Wigan Athletic (again) and Wrexham.

David Lowe (left) watches Jason Dozzell (number ten) challenge the Brighton defence.

Born: Carlisle, 15 October 1960
Signed: 2 October 1978 from apprentice
Debut: *v.* Skied Oslo (UEFA Cup, away), won 3-1
    19 September 1979

Ipswich career:
321 starts (10 subs), 12 goals
Football League: 249(8), 7
Play-offs: 2, 1
FA Cup: 23(10), 1
Football League Cup: 29
UEFA Cup: 15(1), 3
Full Members' Cup: 3
Honours: 1 England B cap, 6 under-21 caps and
    youth international

Other clubs: Sheffield Wednesday, Carlisle
    United (loan), Plymouth Argyle, Torquay
    United and Plymouth Argyle (again).

After Kevin Beattie came from Carlisle, there were high hopes of another youngster from Cumberland discovered by scout John Carruthers. Nicknamed 'Grimace' by his dressing-room colleagues, Steve McCall made his debut in a UEFA Cup first round first leg tie at Skied Oslo.

Once he became established, he accumulated an impressive run of 175 successive first-team appearances between November 1981 and March 1985, which stood as a club record until shattered by Matt Holland. The run ended as a result of suspension after McCall was sent off at Everton in an FA Cup sixth round tie for a challenge on Trevor Steven. It was after the final whistle of this match that Everton manager Harry Catterick collapsed and died. Everton won the replay at Portman Road with a penalty from Graeme Sharp.

McCall moved to Sheffield Wednesday for £300,000 but had rotten luck with injury at Hillsborough, suffering a broken left leg. He played ten games in three seasons as well as half-a-dozen while on loan to Carlisle to help him back to fitness.

The rest of his playing career was spent with Plymouth, Torquay United and Plymouth once again. He acquired some management experience towards the end of his stay in the West Country and has since returned to work with George Burley at Portman Road.

Jimmy McLuckie

Wing-half, 1936 to 1939

The first professionals to join Ipswich Town after the club joined the Southern League in 1936 were Charlie Cowie (later to be reserve team trainer) from Barrow, Jack Blackwell from Boston and Bobby Bruce from Sheffield Wednesday. Then in July, the football world took notice when Jimmy McLuckie, who had played for Scotland only two years earlier, was secured from Aston Villa. He was only twenty-eight years old and in his prime, so it was little wonder that Ipswich turned down offers for him even before he had kicked a ball for the club.

He led Ipswich out in their first ever professional match against Tunbridge Wells Rangers before a crowd of 14,211. The Band of the Scots Guards was present to mark the occasion and there had been a luncheon at the Great White Horse Hotel, at which Stanley Rous and Town chairman, Captain 'Ivan' Cobbold, both spoke.

McLuckie stayed with the club until the start of the Second World War, which marked the end of his career. He was signed by Irish manager Mick O'Brien, who won the Southern League title at the first

Born: Stonehouse, Scotland, 2 April 1908
Died: November 1986
Date signed: 9 July 1936 from Aston Villa
Debut: *v.* Tunbridge Wells Rangers (home), won 4-1, 29 August 1936

Ipswich career;
124 starts, 9 goals
Southern League: 59, 9 goals
Football League: 44, 1
FA Cup: 13, 2
Other matches: 8
Honours: 1 full cap for Scotland in 1934 while with Manchester City

Previous clubs: Hamilton Academicals, Manchester City and Aston Villa.

attempt. O'Brien was then dismissed shortly before the start of the following season because of too close an association with the landlady of a Cobbold pub (The Mulberry Tree) – as a result of which the landlord complained to Captain Cobbold.

Ipswich aimed high as they sought a replacement. They tried in vain for Major Frank Buckley, who was manager of Wolverhampton Wanderers at the time. Instead they secured Adam Scott Duncan, who was the manager of Manchester United. It was Duncan's influence that helped the club gain election to the Football League for the 1938/39 season.

McLuckie remained a key man but, ironically, Tom Fillingham, a central defender from Birmingham City, captained Ipswich in their first-ever League match at home to Southend. Fillingham led the team only twice before McLuckie was put back in charge. When Ipswich were drawn to visit Aston Villa in the third round of the FA Cup he was in his element. He gave a marvellous performance against his old club that helped Ipswich to a 1-1 draw and a replay at Portman Road the following Wednesday afternoon. The tie at Villa Park will be remembered for a mud-throwing incident. There was no score early in the second half when Ipswich were awarded a penalty. Villa full-back Callaghan threw mud at the ball and moved it just as Charlie Fletcher was running up to take the spot-kick, which hit the post. Ipswich lost a dramatic replay 2-1, but Town were now well respected in the Third Division (South). Apart from McLuckie, other experienced players in those early days were goalkeeper Mick Burns, who had played for Preston in the 1937 FA Cup final in the same side as Bill Shankly. Right-back Billy Dale had played for Manchester City in the cup finals of 1933 and 1934 (Dale played in a City team with Frank Swift and Matt Busby).

McLuckie was the first player to be sent off in Town's professional history. He received his marching orders against Guildford City in the Southern League Cup on 2 September 1937. He nevertheless retained the captaincy.

He started his career with Tranent Juniors then helped Hamilton Academicals into the semi-final of the Scottish Cup in the 1931/32 season. He joined Manchester City in 1933 and in December 1934 Aston Villa paid £6,500 to secure his services. He became player-manager of Clacton Town in July 1947. Then he worked for Fisons.

Ipswich Town made their bow in the Football League during the 1938/39 season, with Jimmy McLuckie their best known player. From left to right, back row: G. Alsop, G. Andrews, F. Wheeler, F. Chadwick, F. Shufflebottom, J. Russell. Second row: S. Wright (trainer), W. Dale, R. Rodger, T. Fillingham, M. Burns, D. Daly, H. Sowerbutts, C. Cowie, F. Jones, J. Gorman, O. Parry, R. Thomson (assistant trainer). Third row: T. Morris, B. Davies, J. McLuckie, R.N. Cobbold (director), R.F. Jackson (director), Sir Charles Bunbury (director), Captain J.M. Cobbold (chairman), A. Scott Duncan (secretary-manager), Bt-Col H. Hooper (director), N. Shaw (director), J. Hutcheson, G. Perrett, L. Martin. Front row: J. Cope, J. Little, A. Mulraney, J. McGourty, J. Williams, W. Harris. Trophy: Ipswich and East Suffolk Hospital Cup.

Mick McNeil

Defender, 1964 to 1972

Born: 7 February 1940 at Stockton
Signed: 20 June 1964 from Middlesbrough
Debut: v. Cardiff City (away), 0-0, 22 August 1964

Ipswich career:
168 starts (5 subs), 5 goals
Football League 141 (5) 5 goals
FA Cup: 16
Football League Cup: 11, 1
Honours: 9 full international caps for England in
    1960 and 1961 while with Middlesbrough

Other clubs: Middlesbrough and Cambridge City.

He looked the perfect signing by Jackie Milburn to steady the ship after relegation from the First Division. It appeared too good to be true to sign a twenty-four-year-old defender who had captained the England under-23 side and won 9 full international caps. Furthermore, he had never been on the losing side when playing for his senior national team. He had played in the historic 9-3 victory over Scotland at Wembley in April 1961 alongside Bobby Robson.

It transpired that the reason for his move was that he never saw eye to eye with Raich Carter when he became Boro boss in 1963 and could not get away from Teesside quickly enough. McNeil was still on the Town books when Bobby Robson arrived as manager. Robson had been in the England team in the same 9 games.

McNeil was a dependable character who was natural captaincy material but, after his first two seasons at Portman Road, he was beset by injuries. He seemed dogged by bad luck. He was one of the first players to suffer a gash from the new nylon studs that had been introduced.

On April Fools' Day in 1967, Ipswich were at Northampton. Chris Barnard damaged his shoulder and McNeil came on as substitute and scored the goal in a 1-1 draw. McNeil then went off with a back injury and Dave Harper, a tough wing-half from Millwall, limped off with a leg injury. Only when Ipswich were down to nine men did the Cobblers manage an equaliser. Everyone on the sports desk at the *East Anglian Daily Times* was waiting for Barnard to produce a match-winning performance so they could use the heading

'Chris Barnard puts new heart into Ipswich' – it was topical at the time because of the pioneering surgery by Dr Christian Barnard in South Africa. Sadly, there was never an opportunity to use it.

McNeil captained an FA team sent to the Channel Islands to celebrate an anniversary of the Jersey FA. It was hardly competitive: McNeil's side won 10-0. A qualified coach, McNeil set up a successful chain of sports shops in East Anglia, which kept him name in the public eye long after he had hung up his boots.

Ken Malcolm

Left-back, 1954 to 1964

Born: Aberdeen, 25 August 1926
Signed: 28 May 1954 from Arbroath
Debut: *v.* Hull City (away), lost 2-4,
 4 September 1954

Ipswich career:
293 starts, 2 goals
Football League: 274, 2
FA Cup: 13
Football League Cup: 1
European Cup: 3
Other matches: 2

Other club: Arbroath.

A hard-tackling left-back of the old school, Ken Malcolm came from Scotland in 1954. His versatility was put to good use in his first season when he played a couple of games up front, scoring in a 3-3 draw at Port Vale and in the 5-1 home victory over Doncaster Rovers when Tom Garneys scored four.

Malcolm was signed by Scott Duncan but became an automatic choice under Alf Ramsey. He won a Third Division (South) championship medal in the 1960/61 season and a Second Division championship medal in 1961/62, when he played in all but one of the League games. The only one he missed was against Norwich City at Portman Road just after Christmas.

I always remember the visit to Hull City – who were already relegated with Ipswich safely in mid-table – on the final day of the 1959/60 season. Malcolm had been involved in the fishing industry in Arbroath. He asked me if I would like to get up very early on the Saturday morning (the match day) to see the fish market at Hull. It was an eye-opening experience which confirmed that 'swearing like a fishwife' was no exaggeration. We were both back in the hotel before breakfast. Ipswich lost the match at Boothferry Park 2-0, but there was very little at stake. However, Alf Ramsey would have taken a very dim view of one of his players getting up so early. So far as I know, he never found out.

Malcolm played in only the first three matches of the First Division Championship-winning season, but that included the 4-3 defeat against Burnley at Turf Moor, the most exciting match I have ever seen. He missed the rest of the campaign because of a knee injury that was followed by a serious bout of sciatica. Ramsey converted John Compton, a wing-half signed from Chelsea, to left-back which turned out to be an inspired decision.

Malcolm played in three of Town's four European Cup ties in the autumn of 1962, missing the home victory over AC Milan. After hanging up his boots, he coached the youth squad at Portman Road for a couple of years before a clash of personalities with manager Bill McGarry saw him leave the club. He ran a Suffolk village pub, had a spell as a fish merchant in Aberdeen and then became a hotelier in Guernsey. There he spotted the talent in a young Matt Le Tissier, and tipped off Ipswich Town, but the player opted to spend his career with Southampton. Ken returned to Ipswich in 1985 and was a driver for Fisons until his retirement in July 1991.

Paul Mariner

Centre forward, 1976 to 1984

Born: Bolton, 22 May 1953
Signed: 26 October 1976 from Plymouth Argyle
in a £220,000 deal
Debut: *v.* Manchester United (away), won 1-0,
30 October 1976

Ipswich career:
339 starts, 135 goals
Football League: 260, 96
FA Cup: 31, 19
Football League Cup: 15, 7
UEFA Cup: 28, 12
European Cup Winners' Cup: 4, 1
FA Charity Shield: 1
Honours: 35 England caps (33 while at Ipswich),
2 England B caps

Other clubs: Plymouth Argyle. Arsenal,
Portsmouth, Naxxar Lions and Albany Capitals.

One of the most effective hold-up players in England, he can lay claim to being the classiest centre forward that Ipswich have had on their books. He soon made an impression at Plymouth and Bobby Robson was well aware of his potential and told me off the record that he was monitoring his progress. Perhaps it was just as well that he did.

Ipswich met Bristol City at Ashton Gate when I asked Roger Malone, the *Daily Telegraph* reporter who covered the West Country, if he had seen much of Mariner and what he thought. He said: 'He's travelling to London to sign for West Ham tomorrow'. On Sunday morning I rang Bobby Robson at his home to let him know what was happening. Early that evening, Robson was back on the phone to see

if I could find the home number (ex-directory of course) of Plymouth manager Tony Waiters. Suffice to say, I found the number thanks to my contacts down in Devon. Robson managed to get the West Ham deal stalled by putting in an offer. It was not long before West Bromwich got wind of Mariner's availability to make it a three-club race for his signature. In the end, Ipswich completed the deal with striker Terry Austin and defender John Peddelty going to Plymouth in part exchange. (Unfortunately for Plymouth, Peddelty had suffered a head injury while playing for Ipswich reserves. Another knock in the same place left the medical men advising retirement.)

Mariner was a superstar at Ipswich. He won an FA Cup winner's medal and was a key man in the UEFA Cup triumph over AZ 67 Alkmaar in 1981. He scored 96 goals before moving to Arsenal for £150,000 in February 1994, when Ipswich were needing to raise funds to pay the builders another instalment for the Pioneer Stand – which had been a millstone round the neck of manager Bobby Ferguson.

Later, Mariner played for Portsmouth, Naxxar Lions and Albany Capitals. He did a spot of media work in the North West before returning to the United States to become a coach at the University of Arizona.

Ian Marshall

Centre forward, 1993 and 1996

Born: Liverpool, 20 March 1966
Signed: 9 August 1993 from Oldham Athletic for
 £750,000
Debut: *v.* Oldham Athletic (away), won 3-0,
 14 August 1993

Ipswich career:
92 starts (5 subs), 38 goals
Premiership: 42(5), 13
Football League: 37, 19
FA Cup: 9, 3
Football League Cup: 4, 3

Other clubs: Everton, Oldham Athletic, Leicester
 City, Bolton Wanderers and Blackpool.

Ian Marshall, the only Ipswich Town player who admitted to have suffered injury pushing a supermarket trolley, was an ungainly but dangerous attacker. He opted to join Ipswich from Oldham because Joe Royle wanted him to play in central defence at Boundary Park, while he wanted to prove himself as a goalscorer. Ironically, his debut for Town was against his former club, when he latched onto a long clearance from goalkeeper Clive Baker and scored past Paul Gerrard.

Marshall was Town's leading marksman with 15 goals in the 1993/94 season and scored a real cracker in an FA Cup tie at Swindon after being set up by Stuart Slater. The following season, Ipswich were relegated – sunk almost without trace, despite the fact that Alex Mathie was recruited from Newcastle to form what developed into a highly successful partnership with Marshall in Division One. They scored 37 goals between them, but Ipswich missed out on a place in the play-offs after being held to a goal-less draw by relegated Millwall on the final day of the season at Portman Road.

Marshall moved to Leicester in 1996 for £875,000 as Ipswich

needed, as always, to balance their books. His departure left room for promotion for the likes of James Scowcroft and Richard Naylor from the youth scheme to partner Mathie, who soon afterwards suffered a dislocated shoulder and needed surgery. Marshall spent four years at Leicester, had a brief spell at Bolton and then joined Blackpool. He keeps in touch with his Ipswich colleagues and has been seen back for testimonial golf days and things of that nature.

He rates his best time in football as being at Oldham in 1990 when they reached the final of the Littlewoods Cup and the semi-finals of the FA Cup. Oldham won promotion to the top level of English football the following season. He also recalls a 'great apprenticeship' with Everton.

Paul Mason

Midfield, 1993 to 1997

Born: Liverpool, 3 September 1963
Signed: 18 June 1993 from Aberdeen for £400,000
Debut: *v.* Oldham Athletic (away), won 3-0,
    14 August 1993

Ipswich career:
121 starts (13 subs), 35 goals
Premiership: 37(6), 6
Football League: 66(4), 19
Play-off: 1
FA Cup: 4(3), 3
Football League Cup: 10, 4
Anglo-Italian Cup: 3, 3

Other clubs: Everton, Groningen and Aberdeen.

Paul Mason was something of an unknown quantity so far as Ipswich Town fans were concerned when John Lyall signed him from Aberdeen to boost the fight for survival at the top level. Before he moved to Scotland, he had been playing for Groningen in Holland. He helped the Dons to finish runners-up in the League four times in five years.

Mason was able to score from the wing and was Town's top marksman with 15 goals in 1996/97, after the departure of Ian Marshall to Leicester. There are three goals from Mason that Ipswich fans will have considered extra special. In the 1994/95 season Manchester United, the eventual champions, exuded an air of confidence perhaps to the point of over confidence as they prepared for the match at their overnight HQ of Hintlesham Hall. Ipswich beat them 3-2, with Mason scoring two. Later the same campaign that United gained their revenge in no uncertain manner, administering a 9-0 hammering – and it could have been even more embarrassing but for the goalkeeping of Craig Forrest.

That was the season that Alan Shearer, then with Blackburn, said there were no easy games in the Premiership except against Ipswich. It was all the more pleasing for those at Portman Road that Ipswich should face Blackburn in an FA Cup replay at Ewood Park the following season. The tie went into extra-time when Mason grabbed the winner. Mason recalled: 'Neil Gregory knocked it into my path and I just hit it and it went in. That was a really special moment.'

He scored on his debut for the club at Oldham in August 1993 when Ipswich won 3-0, dribbling the ball round goalkeeper Paul Gerrard. As Ian Marshall was on the mark as well it became the first time in fifty-four years that two players making their debut for the club had scored in the same match.

Mason's best goals, in his opinion, were scored before he came to Ipswich. He was playing for Aberdeen and netted twice in a victory over Rangers in the Skol Cup final. 'That was one of the highlights of my career,' said Mason, who now runs a small but very comfortable hotel in Southport – ideal for Ipswich fans who like to stay overnight for matches in the North West.

Mason's career started as a junior at Everton before he moved to Holland. Aberdeen paid £200,000 for his services, while Ipswich were happy to agree a £400,000 fee when he moved to Portman Road. Mason appeared briefly for Woodbridge Town in the FA Vase, together with John Wark, after he had finished his League career with Ipswich.

Alex Mathie
Forward, 1994 to 1998

Born: Bathgate, 20 December 1968
Signed: 24 February 1995 from Newcastle
    United for £500,000
Debut: *v.* Southampton (home), won 2-1,
    25 February 1995

Ipswich career:
109 starts (22 subs), 47 goals
Premiership: 13, 2
Football League: 77(19), 36
Play-offs: 2
FA Cup: 5(3), 1
Football League Cup: 9, 7
Anglo-Italian Cup: 4, 1
Honours: Scottish youth international

Other clubs: Celtic, Morton, Port Vale, Newcastle
    United, Dundee United and York City.

Strikers hunt in pairs and the Ipswich public enjoyed the partnership between Ian Marshall and Alex Mathie when they scored 37 goals between them in the 1996/97 season in Division One. Mathie collected a hat-trick against Sunderland and looked a good buy at £500,000.

A dislocated shoulder was to upset Mathie's career. At first ultrasound treatment seemed to do the trick, but when he suffered the same problem in a Coca-Cola Cup tie at Crystal Palace in October 1996, it was decided that surgery was the best bet. Furthermore, it was felt to be in the player's interests to have both shoulders repaired, one after the other. That meant a frustratingly long lay-off.

Mathie played 13 matches for Celtic and then moved to Morton, where he hammered in the goals for fun. A loan spell at Port Vale was followed by a £275,000 move to Newcastle, where he was unable to make the big breakthrough he wanted.

Brought up in Falkirk, he became firm friends with Stuart Balmer of Charlton, having played for the same boys' club. The decision to sell Mathie to Dundee United was unpopular with Town fans, who had taken him to their hearts after his first-half hat-trick against Norwich City in February 1998. It was a good decision, though, to let him go as his subsequent contribution at Tannadice Park was disappointing.

Born: Godalming, 4 January 1949
Signed: 3 February 1966 from Portsmouth
Debut: v. Wolverhampton Wanderers, home,
   won 5-2, 7 May 1966

Ipswich career:
737 starts (4 subs), 30 goals
Football League: 588(3), 32
FA Cup: 57, 5
Football League Cup: 43(1), 2
UEFA Cup: 34, 1
European Cup Winners' Cup: 6
Texaco Cup: 8
FA Charity Shield: 1
Honours: 42 England caps, 5 under-23 caps and
   youth international caps

Other clubs: Portsmouth, Southampton. Manager:
   Stoke City, Colchester United. First team
   coach at Sheffield Wed. and Birmingham.

Mick Mills' record speaks for itself. He was a splendid captain with a vast influence, both on and off the field. There is no doubt that Bobby Robson was fortunate to inherit such an excellent professional. Mick used to deliver newspapers to my boarding school at Godalming while he was a lad. He started his football career apprenticed to Portsmouth, but they abandoned their youth policy when managed by George Smith, who had been coach at Portman Road in a turbulent period under Scott Duncan.

Reg Tyrrell, the Ipswich Town chief scout, came from Bournemouth and knew all about Mills. He persuaded him to come to Portman Road to continue his career under Bill McGarry. Mills made his debut when he was 17 years and 123 days old. At the time this was a club record, later to be shattered by goalkeeper Paul Overton (17 years and 11 days) and Jason Dozzell (16 years and 57 days).

Mills was in and out of the side as a teenager under McGarry. Gradually it became clear that Mills was destined to be a star, but even top players have matches they would prefer to forget. Ipswich were in Leipzig in the quarter-finals of the UEFA Cup in March 1974. They travelled behind the Iron Curtain to East Germany with a single goal lead, thanks to Kevin Beattie's 87th-minute goal at Portman Road. It was always going to be touch and go, even though Ipswich had already claimed the scalps of Real Madrid, SS Lazio and FC Twente. Mills was left-back and captain. Five minutes before the interval he was pushed in the face and retaliated. The red card was shown. He could only watch while the remaining ten men defended brilliantly. Leipzig drew level in the 49th minute, Brian Talbot was robbed by the bar, and it ended level after extra-time. Ipswich went out after a penalty shootout.

Next morning I suggested to Mick that we should hire a taxi and get away from it all with a visit to Colditz Castle. It was hardly the escape we had in mind as a great many Town supporters had exactly the same idea. Mills generally kept injury-free and must go down amongst the most dedicated and consistent professionals ever to play for the club. In 1986, after the departure of Bobby Ferguson as manager, Ipswich approached Stoke City for permission to interview Mills. They were turned down because he was under contract at the Victoria Ground. He was amongst those interviewed when George Burley was appointed but was never really in the running at that stage.

Doug Millward

Inside forward, 1955 to 1963

Born: Sheffield, 10 July 1931
Died: December 2000
Signed: 17 June 1955 from Southampton
Debut: v. Norwich City (away), lost 2-3,
    2 April 1956

Ipswich career:
156 appearances, 36 goals
Football League: 143, 35
FA Cup: 10, 1
Football League Cup: 2

Other matches: 1

Doug Millward was talented and very competitive at every sport he played. He was a natural footballer and also a qualified FA coach. After going on specialised courses, Alf Ramsey (who had no coaching badge) would call Millward into his office and pick his brains. Millward played cricket for the RAF and was quickly recruited by Saxmundham. He played tennis – a sport he coached in the United States when his football career was over – for Suffolk. He enjoyed winning and was useful at table-tennis and soon became a top tenpin bowling player as well.

He was a footballer who loved to try the unexpected. When it came off, it looked brilliant. When it failed, he risked having the crowd (and the manager) on his back. He made his debut at Norwich City on the same day as Roy Bailey. He played 35 of the 46 League matches the following season. Between 22 September 1956 and 8 September 1958 he missed just two League matches. In the first of those seasons, he helped provide the ammunition for Ted Phillips – who scored 41 goals in 41 Third Division (South) matches. Hat-tricks at home to Colchester United, Watford and Shrewsbury and away at Reading made Ted a feared man.

Millward lived at 58 All Saints Road, off the Norwich Road. I remember it well because I used to turn up there for my tea almost every Thursday before writing the weekend football previews. His wife, Pat, used to prepare the meal that often preceded a few hands of cards. My Hornby-Dublo electric train set was laid out round his sitting room.

Millward became manager of Poole Town in the Southern League and then moved to St Mirren to become that rarity – an English manager in the Scottish League. While there the Saints won at Celtic with a goal from Frank Treacy, also a former Ipswich player. Millward phoned me to say: 'Frank scored the winner. Then he had to go to confession.' Treacy was a Catholic scoring against Celtic.

It was next stop the United States, where the anticipated football boom never really happened. Instead he turned his attention to coaching tennis. His son, Doug junior, has followed in his father's tennis footsteps.

Millward died in the United States and his ashes were brought to England and scattered on the Solent, where he had been involved in an air-sea rescue operation while on National Service.

Simon Milton was already twenty-three years old when he was signed by Ipswich Town from Bury Town. Bobby Ferguson had set up the deal before leaving the club. John Duncan went ahead with the signing and never regretted taking on a winger with an eye for goal. He had loan spells down in Devon with Exeter City and Torquay United, before breaking into the Ipswich first team in the spring of 1988. The following year he had the chance to join Norwich City, convenient from his Thetford home, but opted for a new deal at Portman Road instead.

In December 1988 he won over Town fans by scoring the extra-time winner against Norwich City in the Simod Cup at Portman Road. The Canaries went down 1-0, their feathers suitably ruffled.

He had a knack of scoring at Portsmouth, usually at the Milton Road end. He scored two in a 3-2 victory over Pompey on 28 October 1989, beating Alan Knight with

Born: Fulham, 23 August 1963
Signed: 17 July 1987 from Bury Town for £5,000
Debut: *v.* Swindon Town (away), lost 2-4,
    28 December 1987

Ipswich career:
258 starts (72 subs) 56
Premiership 37(15), 5
Football League: 180(49), 44
FA Cup: 12, 1
Football League Cup: 15(7), 3
Anglo-Italian Cup: 4, 1
Full Members' Cup: 10(1), 2

Other clubs: Exeter City (loan) and Torquay
    United (loan).

a rasping drive and then firing home a second after being set up by David Lowe. He was the supporters' Player of the Year for the 1995/96 season.

Doug Moran

Inside right, 1961 to 1964

Born: Musselburgh, 27 July 1934
Signed: 11 July 1961 from Falkirk
Debut: *v.* Bolton Wanderers (away), draw 0-0,
    22 August 1961

Ipswich career:
123 starts, 37 goals
Football League: 104, 31 goals
FA Cup: 7, 1
Football League Cup: 7, 3
European Cup: 4, 2
FA Charity Shield: 1

Dapper Doug Moran joined Ipswich Town at just the right time. Alf Ramsey paid £12,000 to Falkirk and knew he had secured a bargain. Alf commented: 'If I had £30,000 to spend I could not find a player so useful to the club as Moran.'

Moran gained the Scottish Leaving Certificate (corresponding to GCE) at Musselburgh Grammar School. He signed as a part-timer for Hibernian at the age of seventeen, but found himself in competition with the brilliant Scottish international star Bobby Johnstone. In 1956 he went on loan to Falkirk and joined them for £1,500 at the end of the season. The following year he scored the winning goal in extra-time that saw Falkirk beat Kilmarnock in the Scottish Cup final. Nicknamed 'Dixie' at Portman Road, Moran was one of those players often seen doing voluntary extra training – working on weight-lifting or sprinting.

When he turned up at the players' reunion to mark the fortieth anniversary of winning the Championship, Moran recalled the day I drove him to an FA Cup third round tie at Mansfield. All I remember is that there was snow on the ground, Jimmy Leadbetter scored a hat-trick and Mansfield had just bought the grandstand from Hurst Park racecourse. I cannot imagine why my driving should have made such a lasting impression on Mr Moran!

In that period, Musselburgh was a hotbed for star footballers. John White of Tottenham and Scotland (who was later killed by lightning on the golf course) lived in the same street as Moran, so both were able to show off Championship medals.

After the disastrous season of 1963/64 under Jackie Milburn, Moran returned to his native land to play for Dundee United. It was little consolation to him that he had scored two goals against Manchester United at Portman Road in September 1963: Ipswich crashed 7-2.

His golf handicap while at Ipswich was five. He won the Southern Area professional footballers' championship and came fifth in the all-England final. It was no great surprise that he should return to win the ex-players reunion tournament at Waldringfield Heath, but a few eyebrows were raised when he turned up with a handicap of twenty-one! A good swing seldom disappears.

Moran was a players' player: much of his hard work was perhaps never fully appreciated by the fans.

Peter Morris

Wing-half, 1968 to 1974

Born: North Houghton, 8 November 1943
Signed: 1 March 1968 from Mansfield Town
Debut: *v.* Derby County (away), won 3-2,
    2 March 1968

Ipswich career:
249 starts (9 subs), 16 goals
Football League: 213(7), 13
FA Cup: 15
Football League Cup: 8(2)
UEFA Cup: 6(1)
Texaco Cup: 7, 2

Other clubs: Mansfield Town, Norwich City,
    Mansfield Town (again) and Peterborough.

Peter Morris joined the Ipswich Town promotion drive back into the First Division in March 1968. He cost £12,000 from Mansfield Town, where he had been one of the youngest captains in the Stags' history. His presence in the final fourteen matches, together with that of £30,000 striker John O'Rourke from Middlesbrough, saw a dramatic upturn in Town's fortunes. Nine of the final matches were won and the other five drawn. Ipswich ended on top of the table, but only a single point ahead of QPR and Blackpool.

Morris was an ideal type of reliable professional for Bobby Robson to inherit. His passing was extremely accurate and he picked up the occasional goal.

The Texaco Cup may have seemed a bit of an ordeal when the first round was a two-leg affair against St Johnstone, the first leg being in Perth. (There was no train link to get me there in time so I drove to Perth, reported on the match, and drove straight back. I was so tired by the time I reached Newcastle that I parked the car under the Tyne Bridge and slept for a few hours.) Ipswich were 4-2 ahead, so the second leg attracted very little interest in Suffolk, only 5,500 turning out to see Ipswich beat the Scots 2-0. Victories over Wolverhampton and then Newcastle United, both over two legs, led to an East Anglian final with Norwich City. This is just what the sponsors wanted. Ipswich won the first leg 2-0 with both goals coming from Morris in front of 29,700. Norwich still fancied their chances, however, and 35,798 were packed into Carrow Road. This time Ipswich won 2-1, with Norfolk boys Trevor Whymark and Clive Woods getting the goals to silence the Canaries.

It has been a standing joke between Morris and myself that he still has one of my Old Carthusian cricket sweaters from the days he played for Saxmundham. He was a useful slow-medium bowler who maintained a nagging length. The sweater must be pretty threadbare by now.

He became first-team coach at Newcastle United under Bill McGarry. Then followed various managerial appointments, including Mansfield Town (1976-78), Peterborough (1979-82), Crewe Alexandra (1982-83 before Dario Gradi started his long reign), Southend United (1983-84) and non-League posts at King's Lynn and Kettering Town.

Tony Mowbray
Centre half, 1995 to 2000

Born: Saltburn, 22 November 1963
Signed: 6 October 1996 from Celtic for £300,000
Debut: *v.* Wolverhampton Wanderers (home),
    lost 1-2, 7 October 1995

Ipswich career:
150 starts (3 subs), 8 goals
Football League: 125(3), 5
Play-offs: 6, 1
FA Cup: 9
Football League Cup: 7, 1
Anglo-Italian Cup: 3, 1
Honours: England B

Other clubs: Middlesbrough and Celtic.

Tony Mowbray's final appearance for Ipswich Town was like a dream come true. He captained the team to victory in the Division One play-off final against Barnsley at Wembley. To put icing on the cake, he headed home Town's 28th-minute equaliser from a left-wing cross from Jim Magilton. Then, with Ipswich back in the Premiership, he hung up his boots and turned his attention to coaching.

'Mogga' had been a lifelong Middlesbrough fan. He was born in Teesside on the day President Kennedy was assassinated. He was captain of Middlesborough FC at a time when the club looked as though it might go out of existence. It was the summer of 1986 when the famous club, that had hosted group matches in the 1966 World Cup only twenty years previously, was in a deep depression. When the Boro players turned up for pre-season training there was a security guard on the locked gates. The club had stopped paying the players. The PFA stepped in to provide the money so essential to those with families.

Manager Bruce Rioch buckled down to the task even though training was in the local park with shirts thrown down as goalposts. Even the balls used in training were borrowed.

Gates had dropped to little over 3,000 the previous season, but 'Mogga' was the captain with Gary Pallister alongside him. The battling spirit was there, and that may have been what persuaded Steve Gibson to form a consortium that has seen such a spectacular recovery.

Middlesbrough were back in a healthy state by the time Mowbray moved to Celtic, where he suffered the heartbreak of losing his young wife, Bernadette, to cancer. It was a terrible time for him, but his character shone through. A bad groin strain sustained on an icy night at Sunderland's Roker Park took time to heal. Once he was back in harness, Mowbray became a leader on the field and a wise adviser to young players off it.

In the Division One promotion season, Mowbray was only planning to play in a crisis. That crisis happened in the form of poor results, so Ipswich incorporated Mowbray's cool head at the back – although it meant operating a sweeper system.

'Mogga' looked quite at home with his part in the victory at Wembley – one of the pinnacles of his long career. It was certainly the match watched and appreciated by most Ipswich fans. There were those that felt Mowbray would be able to hold his own in the Premiership as well, but he decided to end his playing career on a high.

Arnold Muhren

Midfield, 1978 to 1982

Bobby Robson's Ipswich side won the FA Cup in 1978, but the manager knew it was time to rebuild. The following summer he introduced Arnold Muhren and what a difference it made. He cost only £150,000, although there was a clause that he could leave for nothing at the end of his contract. The deal was by no means easy to complete, because Mrs Muhren was at first none too keen on leaving Holland. It took all Robson's powers of persuasion. All was well in the end.

With Muhren, and later Frans Thijssen, in the side Ipswich played less of the long ball. They tried to work through the midfield and became one of the most respected and attractive sides in Europe.

The pity was that the lack of depth in the squad, combined with a hectic programme, cost them the League title when they were undoubtedly a far better side than eventual Championship winners Aston Villa were at the time.

Muhren combined especially well with young Scot Alan Brazil. The cliché about a 'cultured left foot' was used time and again about Muhren. It was an accurate description. He was a key man in the glorious UEFA Cup run of 1981 and then, when his job at Portman Road was done, he joined Manchester United. On his return to Holland he became a respected coach.

Born: Holland, 2 June 1951
Signed: 15 August 1978 from FC Twente for £150,000
Debut: v. Liverpool (home), lost 0-3, 22 August 1978

Ipswich career:
214 starts, 29 goals
Football League: 161, 21
FA Cup: 19, 3
Football League Cup; 15, 2
UEFA Cup: 17, 3
European Cup Winners' Cup: 2
Honours: Holland international, winning 6 caps while at Ipswich

Other clubs: FC Twente and Manchester United.

Arnold Muhren appears on the far right of the picture.

Andy Nelson
Centre half, 1959 to 1964

Born: Canning Town, 5 July 1935
Date signed: 27 May 1959 from West Ham United
Debut: *v.* Huddersfield Town (home), lost 1-4,
    22 August 1959

Ipswich career:
215 starts, goals 0
Football League: 193
FA Cup: 11
Football League Cup: 7
European Cup: 3
FA Charity Shield: 1

Other clubs: West Ham United, Leyton Orient
    and Plymouth Argyle.

Andy Nelson was signed by Alf Ramsey to bolster the Ipswich defence. He was the fifth child in a family of eight, born in the vicinity of the West Ham ground. He won an Army Cup winners' medal with 4th Training Battery REME in 1957, receiving the trophy from the Queen. He played only 15 games for the Hammers as a part-timer before joining Ipswich in May 1959. His father had insisted that he served a five-year apprenticeship as a marine engineer on London Docks in addition to undergoing National Service. He was unable to displace Ken Brown as the regular West Ham centre-half, so the chance of a move to Portman Road was more than welcome.

He played his first full season under the captaincy of Reg Pickett, but started 1960/61 season as the undisputed Town skipper. A solid defender in the old style, he never managed to score a first-team goal for the club. Recognised by Ramsey as a natural leader, Nelson had the respect of his colleagues.

I recall a Friday night in Manchester when I took my car on the trip North and stayed at the team hotel. Ramsey liked to take the Ipswich players to the cinema on the night before a game after making the trip by train earlier in the day. Nelson and Ted Phillips knew I had the car and said: 'Let's sit behind Alf in the cinema and, when the lights go out, slip away. We can then drive out of town, have a pint, and get back to the hotel before the cinema comes out.' I had no objection to this plan.

As luck would have it we stopped at a pub at random only to find there were a couple of West Ham players in there who were due to play at Bolton the following afternoon. We all had a pint, a game of darts, and then returned in good time to the hotel. Alf, who missed very little, probably guessed what had happened. He never made an issue of it and merely said: 'So you didn't like the film then, Andy?' just to let the skipper know that his absence had been duly noted.

Andy broke his nose in the European Cup tie against Floriana in Malta, but was generally fairly free of serious injury. After leaving Ipswich, Nelson played for Leyton Orient and then Plymouth Argyle. After his playing career ended, he became manager of Gillingham and Charlton Athletic. He subsequently worked for Charlton's commercial department before emigrating to Spain, where he plays bowls to a high standard. He returned to Ipswich for the fortieth anniversary of the 1961/62 Championship success.

Roger Osborne

Midfield, 1971 to 1981

Born: Otley (Suffolk), 9 March 1950
Signed: 12 October 1971 from juniors
Debut: *v.* Wolverhampton Wanderers (home), won 2-0, 27 October 1973

Ipswich career:
127 starts (22 subs), 10 goals
Football League: 109(15), 9
FA Cup: 8(4), 1
Football League Cup: 2(1)
UEFA Cup: 8(2)

Other club: Colchester United.

Roger Osborne's winning goal against Arsenal in the 1978 FA Cup final will never be forgotten by Ipswich Town supporters. He latched onto a slip by Willie Young and cracked the ball into the net past Pat Jennings. The blue-and-white end of Wembley Stadium went delirious with delight. Osborne was then overcome by a mixture of exhaustion, joy and emotion. He left the stage having made history. On came a fresh Mick Lambert to finish the match. It was a fairytale for a lad from Otley, not far from Ipswich.

One national newspaper jumped to the conclusion that he came from the Otley in Yorkshire and had a heading 'Eee By Gum'. Explaining why he left the field at Wembley, Osborne said: 'It was a culmination of two things mainly, the intense atmosphere through the heat and possibly the fact that there was a lack of oxygen after being engulfed by my team mates.'

It is ironic that a week before the cup final it looked as though Osborne might not be selected. Bobby Robson had it in mind to recall Colin Viljoen after a long lay-off through injury. He envisaged a classic midfield tussle between Viljoen and Liam Brady. The week before Wembley, Ipswich crashed 6-1 against Aston Villa at Villa Park with Viljoen recalled to the team. The other players made their feelings clear – Osborne was immensely popular in the dressing room. The other lads wanted him in and Robson decided that was after all the best plan.

Osborne had the concentration and determination to mark top players out of the game. One night at Stoke he hardly allowed Alan Hudson, the former Chelsea star, a kick. More famously, he tamed the great Johann Cruyff when Barcelona came to Portman Road for a UEFA Cup tie in 1976.

A real grafter, Osborne forced his way into professional football through the back door. He had been taking his brother David to training at Portman Road when, rather than just hang around, he was invited to join in. His potential was spotted and he certainly made the most of his opportunity. One wonders how many others in local football could make the grade if given the chance.

The most embarrassing moment in Osborne's career at Portman Road came when a burglar stole all he could reach by putting his arm through a dressing room window. Osborne's false teeth had been in his top pocket. Maybe they will turn up one day in a memorabilia auction.

Russell Osman
Central defender, 1976 to 1985

Born: Repton, 14 February 1959
Signed: 8 March 1976 from apprentice
Debut: *v.* Chelsea (home), won 1-0,
    3 September 1977

Ipswich career:
382 starts (3 subs), 21 goals
Football League: 294, 17
FA Cup: 30(2), 1
Football League Cup: 28, 3
UEFA Cup: 23(1)
European Cup Winners' Cup: 6
FA Charity Shield: 1
Honours: 11 caps for England, 2 B caps and
    7 under-21 caps. (He was also an England
    schoolboy rugby international)

Other clubs: Leicester City, Southampton,
    and Bristol City.

Russell Osman, son of Rex who played a couple of League games for Derby County in the 1953/54 season, turned his attention to football and joined the list of top-class central defenders to emerge through the Ipswich youth system. He was unlucky not to play in the 1978 FA Cup final after turning out in 28 of the First Division matches that season as well as the cup ties at Cardiff, Bristol Rovers (home) and Millwall.

He must have learned plenty from playing alongside Allan Hunter at the start of his career. Then he had a spell as partner to the legendary Kevin Beattie before forming a tremendous understanding with Terry Butcher. Osman and Butcher were rocks in defence in that UEFA Cup run of 1980/81. He also played in the anti-climax the following season, when Ipswich went out against an Aberdeen side who were managed by Alex Ferguson.

Osman was a natural games player. He became involved in coaching and management with Bristol City and Cardiff City. He also tried his hand at media work both on radio and television. Apart from Ian Cranson, he was just about the last of the home-produced central defenders for some years, Ipswich having to go into the transfer market to secure his successors like David Linighan, Brian Gayle and Tony Mowbray.

Tommy Parker

Wing half and inside forward, 1946 to 1957

Born: Hartlepool, 13 February 1924
Died: 18 March 1996
Signed: 9 November 1946 when amateur
Debut: v. Norwich City (home), won 5-0,
    7 September 1946

Ipswich career:
474 starts, 95 goals
Football League: 428, 86 goals
FA Cup: 37, 7
Other matches: 10, 2

He was one of Town's greatest leaders on the field, even in times of adversity. In the supporters' handbook for the 1955/56 season, following relegation from the Second Division after their first campaign at that level, an unknown author (with a style suspiciously like former *EADT* sports editor Alan Everett) wrote: 'Parker's leadership as captain of the side was a great feature of the season. The example he set, both on and off the field, must have been a continual source of inspiration to the team around him.'

The previous year, when Ipswich were Third Division (South) champions for the first time, it was written: 'Full praise must be given to Parker as captain of the team. A greater captain Ipswich never had. His wholehearted endeavour and infectious enthusiasm won him the hearts of all. Here was a player who could turn a match on his own. While his team might be drooping in despair, Parker, with refound energy, would drive himself forward and fight the other team single-handed. In success or failure he was equally great.'

Perhaps that was a bit over the top, but it gives an indication of the role he played at Portman Road in those days. Parker first turned out for Ipswich in the transitional 1945/46 season after the Second World War. He was in the Royal Navy at Shotley and scored a couple of goals in his first game, a 2-3 defeat at Watford. These matches did not count in the records and he was still an amateur. He was signed as a professional in the 1946/47 season, the first proper League

campaign since 1938/39. He made 40 or more League appearances in nine of his eleven full seasons and 36 in one of the others. His most spectacular campaign came in 1955/56, when he moved up front and cracked in 30 goals in 44 games – setting a captain's example alongside either Tom Garneys or Ron Blackman, who had been a prolific marksman in his days with Reading FC.

Despite his powers of leadership, Parker was twice involved in FA Cup ties when a chastened Ipswich left the field with red faces. In January 1955, the amateurs of Bishop Auckland came to Portman Road in the third round, coached by Jock Sowerby, who had played for Ipswich as amateur in the 1930s. I recall watching the game as a schoolboy on the terraces in front of the old wooden stand that ended up at Foxhall Stadium (until blown down in gales). The tie ended in a 3-3 draw, with Ipswich crashing out in the replay in the snowy North East. They played matches in those days in conditions that would never even be considered possible today.

Parker held the club appearance record until overhauled by Mick Mills, another of the club's greatest captains. Perhaps Parker's worst moment with the club came in the close season on 26 July 1953 when he was travelling back from a charity cricket match at Gorleston in a Land Rover loaned from director John Cobbold, who was later to become chairman. The vehicle overturned at Yoxford, but Parker escaped lightly compared with Don Green, George Clarke and Ted Pole who were all out of football for a considerable while. Manager Scott Duncan never approved of players having cars of their own. Maybe he had a point.

Bobby Petta
Winger, 1996 to 1999

Born: Rotterdam, 6 August 1974
Signed: 29 June 1996
Debut: *v.* Manchester City (away), lost 0-1,
    18 August 1996

Ipswich career:
71 starts (18 subs), 9 goals
Football League: 55(15), 9
Play-offs: 3
FA Cup: 5(1)
Football League Cup: 8(2)
Honours: Holland schoolboy, youth and
    under-21 caps

Other clubs: Feyenoord and Celtic.

Bobby Petta showed plenty of skill on the left wing, but his contract was starting to run out by the time he was starting to make the necessary adjustment to cope with the pace and stamina requirements of English League football. Ipswich realised they were about to lose him on a Bosman free transfer. Town made a desperate attempt to set up a cut-price deal with Barnsley, but Petta took the advice of his agents and stayed put. He had one agent in Holland and another in Britain.

The plan was clear in his mind. He was to move in the summer of 1999 on a free transfer so that he could negotiate more favourable personal terms. He ended with Celtic just at a time that the Parkhead club were ending a long period of Rangers dominance. Petta impressed the Glaswegian fans but, as at Ipswich, he had a succession of niggling injury problems, which must have been frustrating for manager Martin O'Neill.

He and Danny Sonner arrived in Ipswich within days of one another. Sonner came from Preussen Cologne on the recommendation of former England star Tony Woodcock. Petta was highly rated by Town scout Romeo Zondervan, having played representative football in Holland at schools, youth and under-21 level.

His early days at Ipswich were difficult. He admitted: 'I found it very hard. I would just go home and sleep after every training session to try to get some energy back.' At the time he was staying with fellow Dutchman Gus Uhlenbeek and his family. In his first season with the club he started only a single League match.

Petta tended to shine on one half and become quiet in the other. Maybe that was an illusion. I felt sorry for him, though, at Grimsby when he was tripped in the penalty area. No penalty was awarded and, to add insult to injury, he was shown a yellow card for diving. Referees do their best but are wrong far too often.

What would Ted Phillips be worth in today's transfer market? How much would they pay him a week? Certainly he would have had no need to lay cables to make a living once his football career was over. In his prime, he possessed the most powerful shot in football. Ted would let fly from 30 yards. Sometimes the ball would scream into the net. Other times it would be blocked and that ace predator Ray Crawford would score from the rebound. There were times, too, when supporters halfway back in Churchmans or the North Stand would duck hurriedly!

Phillips and Crawford hunted as a pair. When Crawford was picked for England in 1962, there is no doubt in my mind that Phillips should have played alongside him. An impressive 41 goals in as many games in the 1956/57 season saw Ipswich as champions of the Third Division (South). He scored 30 goals in 40 games when the Second Division title was won. At the top level he scored 28 goals in 40 games, which was

Born: Leiston 21 August 1933
Signed: 11 December 1953 from Leiston Town
Debut: *v.* Watford, away, lost 0-1, 3 March 1954

Ipswich career;
295 starts, 161 goals
Football League: 269, 161
FA Cup: 12, 9
Football League Cup: 7, 5
European Cup: 3, 4
FA Charity Shield: 1, 0
Other matches: 3, 2

Other clubs: Leyton Orient, Luton Town and Colchester United. He then became player-coach of Floriana in Malta.

also an amazing record, especially as Crawford scored 33 in 41 games. No wonder Ipswich Town were champions.

Ted Phillips blasts a left-footed penalty kick past Arsenal's Welsh international goalkeeper Jack Kelsey at Portman Road. Ted could kick equally hard with either foot.

Ted is perhaps just as famous for his practical jokes. He once filled Jimmy Forsyth's medical bag with nuts and bolts that he found on King's Cross Station. He almost cleared a crowded London Underground train in rush hour with most convincing shouts of 'all change'.

He won a bet with chairman John Cobbold when he ran out for a Boxing Day match against Leicester City in 1961 wearing a ginger wig. It was not the sort of prank that amused Ramsey. It confused many Town fans, who thought there had been a new signing.

There were times when Alf Ramsey planned training without a ball, but Ted usually had one hidden away somewhere. It was often to be found deep in the heap of coke that was there to heat the water.

Ted was a lethal fast bowler, who played for Suffolk in the Minor Counties. He caused consternation and was reported to Lord's by an umpire with a limited sense of humour after he bowled a red apple instead of the ball to start the day's play. Alf used to allow me to do a spot of training in the afternoons at Portman Road. One day I agreed to let Ted take penalties against me on the practice pitch. A couple had whistled past me into the net when Alf looked out of his office window, a wooden hut, and shouted: 'Stop that at once, Ted. You'll kill him.'

I once felt the force of a Phillips shot in my midriff when I was allowed to keep goal in a seven-a-side match on the Manchester City training ground. Ted was on my side and, when I was expecting a pass back, he rifled the ball at full pace. This gave me the experience first hand of the 'magic sponge' and smelling salts. I recall Alf's team talk after that training session, the only one I was ever privileged to hear. He was preparing the team for the match at Burnley after the 0-0 draw at Bolton on the opening day of the season. It was so inspiring that even I felt I could have done well at Turf Moor that Tuesday night.

When Ted had the ball at his feet within 30 yards of goal there was a hush of anticipation in the crowd. Goalkeepers trembled and one even turned his back on a shot. There was, however, inevitable wear and tear on Ted's knees and now he has steel kneecaps. These set off the security alarms whenever he travels by air.

Alf often made the players walk from the railway station to the ground on match days to loosen them up after the trip. This gave Ted the chance of slipping into a pub for a beer. I remember at Lincoln it was my job to keep watch at the pub door and give him a signal if Alf or trainer Jimmy Forsyth were about.

When the Saxmundham cricketers visited Castle Park, the home of Colchester & East Essex, Ted gave us an especially warming welcome. He was not playing that day but was it a chilly afternoon and he thought it would help the visitors, who were batting second, if a very stiff whisky was mixed with their tea. No one complained, but it did have an adverse effect on the score. I still don't know if anyone paid the bar bill.

Characters like Ted do not seem to exist in present-day football – more is the pity. Leiston Town manager Ian Gillespie certainly did Ipswich a big favour when he pointed out Ted's talents to Ipswich manager Scott Duncan. In Ted's time they prepared for matches with steak rather than pasta and, in occasional cases, perhaps a pint. It seemed to work pretty well.

Reg Pickett

Right half, 1957 to 1963

Born: Bareilly, India, 6 January 1927
Signed: 19 July 1957 from Portsmouth
Debut: *v.* Blackburn Rovers (away), drawn 0-0,
    24 August 1957

Ipswich career:
148 starts, 4 goals
Football League: 140, 3
FA Cup: 4, 0
Football League Cup: 1, 0
European Cup: 1, 0
Other matches: 2, 1

Other club: Portsmouth.

Reg Pickett enjoyed nine successful years with Portsmouth, where he won a First Division Championship medal in 1949. He was thirty-one years old when Alf Ramsey decided this his experience at the top level was just what Ipswich needed to help them consolidate in the Second Division. Relegated immediately the previous time they had reached such heights, Ipswich had learned their lesson. They planned to take no chances.

Born in India, where his father was in the Army, Reg returned to England and represented his school in Reading. At the age of seventeen he joined the Royal Navy and was involved in the final year of the Second World War.

In 1947 he played for Weymouth in the Western League. Eighteen months later he was on the staff at Fratton Park alongside such illustrious names as Jimmy Dickinson, Jack Froggatt and Peter Harris. Although Doug

Rees remained as Ipswich Town captain for a while, Pickett took over the mantle at the start of November, although Rees remained in the side. Rees had fallen out with Alf Ramsey. It turned out to be the solid Welshman's farewell season.

Pickett led Ipswich in the 2-0 FA Cup fourth round defeat against Manchester United at Old Trafford. It turned out to be the last home game played by the Busby Babes before the Munich air disaster. The United team against Ipswich was: Gregg, Foulkes, Byrne, Colman, Jones, Edwards, Morgans, Charlton, Taylor, Viollet and Scanlon. Of that side, Byrne, Colman, Jones, Edwards and Taylor lost their lives, together with reserves Geoff Bent, Billy Whelan and David Pegg.

Athough Baxter took over from Pickett midway through the Second Division championship campaign of 1960/61, Ramsey held the former Pompey man in high regard. He called on his vast experience in the European Cup second round tie away to AC Milan in the San Siro Stadium, despite the fact that he had played in only a handful of first-team matches in nearly two years. Ipswich went down 3-0 in persistent rain against a side that had such world-class stars as Cesare Maldini, Giovanni Trapattoni, Gianni Rivera and Jose Altafini.

After ending his career with Stevenage Town, he returned to live in the Portsmouth area and then worked in the taxi business for some years.

Trevor Putney
Midfield, 1980 to 1986

Born: Harold Hill, 9 April 1960
Signed: 15 September 1980 from Brentwood
    Town
Debut: *v.* Arsenal (home), lost 0-1,
    9 October 1982

Ipswich career:
118 starts (9 subs), 9 goals
Football League: 94(9), 8
FA Cup: 9
Football League Cup: 15, 1

Other clubs: Norwich City, Middlesbrough,
    Watford and Leyton Orient.

The chirpy Essex lad was voted Town's Player of the Year in 1983/84 season. The supporters liked his work rate and cheerful demeanour. Manager Bobby Ferguson jokingly said it must have been his blond hair that won him the votes.

Signed from Brentwood Town, he soon made an impact at Portman Road and may remain best known for one of his pranks. He had gone into partnership with goalkeeper Mark Grew in a second-hand shop in St Peter's Street. Grew was in goal for the reserves at Portman Road when Putney got onto the tannoy during the match. When Grew fielded a backpass there was the message, loud and clear: 'Well played Barney. See you in L'Aristos tonight.' Barney was Grew's nickname and the meeting place in question was a nightclub in Colchester. Bobby Ferguson, watching the match from the directors' box, at once recognised the Essex accent. He raced to the tannoy room and caught Putney at the scene. It took Ferguson several years before he could see the funny side of what happened.

Once, after being sent off at Newcastle, Putney decided to make his own way home. He did not relish the thought of an ear-bashing from the manager all the way back on the team coach.

Putney moved to Norwich in a swap with experienced striker John Deehan. The fans missed Putney, who now comes to Portman Road from time to time as a statistician for the Press Association (who nowadays use former professional footballers for this job).

Billy Reed

Winger, 1953 to 1958

Billy Reed (left) training with inside forward Alex Crowe from St Mirren.

Born: Rhondda, 25 January 1928
Signed: 14 July 1953 from Brighton
Debut: v. Walsall (away), won 2-0, 19 August 1953

Ipswich career;
169 starts, 46 goals
Football League: 155, 43
FA Cup: 13, 3
Honours: 2 caps for Wales

Other clubs: Cardiff City, Brighton & Hove Albion,
    Swansea Town and Worcester City.

The arrival of right-winger Billy Reed at Portman Road from Brighton for £1,750 was good for Ipswich Town and for the player. Scott Duncan's inspired signings of Reed, left-winger George McLuckie from Blackburn and inside-right Alex Crowe from St Mirren transformed a mediocre side into champions of the Third Division (South). The club they pipped for promotion was Brighton, Reed's former employers.

It was not long before Reed, who revelled on the perfect pitch provided by groundsman Freddie Blake, was being described as 'the Stanley Matthews of the Third Division'. His dribbling ability certainly was impressive and he had an eye for goal as well. News of his good form reached the headquarters of the Welsh Football Association. He was picked to play for Wales against Scotland and Yugoslavia in 1955. He became the first player to win a full cap while on the Town's books.

In January 1957, Reed was directly involved in one of the most controversial incidents in Ipswich Town's history. An FA Cup third round tie with Second Division Fulham, who included Johnny Haynes, was nearing its end. Fulham led 3-2 with an 85th-minute goal. With the seconds ticking away, Tom Garneys crossed from the left and Reed knocked the ball into the net. Referee Ken Stokes blew his whistle at just about the same time, so no one knew the outcome of the match. Manager Alf Ramsey had no idea of the final score until after he had visited the referee's dressing room. It transpired that Mr Stokes had blown his whistle a split second before the ball entered the net so Ipswich had been beaten. A crowd massed outside the changing rooms. The club was subsequently reprimanded by the FA for the misconduct of their supporters – which seemed a bit tough.

In 1958, Reed returned to his native Wales to play for Swansea Town, who paid £3,000 (so Ipswich made a profit). Peter Berry became the Town's regular outside-right the following season. He was younger brother to Manchester United's John Berry, who was unconscious several weeks after the Munich air disaster. In 1959/60, Peter's career was ended when he wrenched his left ankle in a home match against Lincoln. On his comeback against West Ham reserves he suffered severe damage to his knee ligaments in a tackle by John Lyall.

Reed lived and worked in Swansea. He spent fourteen years as a laboratory technician for Ashland (UK) Ltd and then as a commissionaire at the Swansea Guildhall until his retirement in 1994.

Doug 'Dai' Rees

Centre half, 1949 to 1959

Born: Slyne, near Neath 12 February 1923
Died: February 2000
Signed: 12 February 1949 from Treodyrhin
Debut: v. Leyton Orient (away), drawn 1-1,
    9 April 1949

Ipswich career:
387 starts, 1 goal
Football League: 356, 1
FA Cup: 29
Ipswich Hospital Cup: 1
Norfolk Jubilee Cup: 1
Honours: Welsh amateur international

He was twenty-six years old when he arrived at Portman Road from Treodyrhin, who received a £350 donation. He took over from George Rumbold on his debut and soon became an automatic choice at the heart of the defence in place of Dave Bell until Alf Ramsey's time. He was club captain in the days when the players all turned up for training on bicycles. Even as skipper it did not pay to argue with Ramsey. Dai questioned a decision and quickly dropped out of favour, although he was in his mid-thirties at the time.

Centre-halves were stoppers in those days. They were not expected to score goals. His only strike came in a 2-2 draw at Shrewsbury, when he was deputising up front on a day when George Clarke was centre-half. He later played for Sudbury Town and became player-coach at Halstead Town in June 1966. He was succeeded for a short spell by Vic Snell, who was a Suffolk-born lad who had spent many years in the reserves. Snell opened the church fete at Kelsale in 1959. After leaving Ipswich he then emigrated to South Africa. Rees worked for William Browns, timber merchants, until suffering a stroke in 1982.

A late starter in professional football because of the Second World War, 'Dai' was one of the many players to emerge from the Welsh Valleys to do a stalwart job in the Football League. He was first-team captain, but was one of the few players to fall foul of Alf Ramsey.

Jimmy Robertson

Right-winger, 1970 to 1972

Bobby Robson made a £95,000 transfer swoop just before the transfer deadline in March 1970 that enabled the club to rise clear of the very real threat of relegation from the First Division. In came right-winger Jimmy Robertson from Arsenal and centre forward Frank Clarke from QPR. There were seven matches to play and the relegation issue was in the melting pot. Sheffield Wednesday, Sunderland, Ipswich Town and Crystal Palace had two points separating them.

The first match for the new duo was at home to Sunderland. A 2-0 victory, a real 'four pointer', was just what was needed to boost morale. Nine points were collected out of a possible fourteen and Ipswich rose to the safety of eighteenth place in the table. Robertson scored in a 2-0 home win against Southampton and bagged two in the 3-2 victory over runners-up Leeds United in the final match of the season.

Robertson started his career with Cowdenbeath and won an amateur cap for his country. His next stop was St Mirren, where sparkling

Born: Glasgow, 17 December 1944
Signed: 21 March 1970 from Arsenal for £55,000
Debut: *v.* Sunderland (home), won 2-0,
    21 March 1970

Ipswich career:
98 starts, 12 goals
Football League: 87, 10
FA Cup: 8, 1
Football League Cup: 3, 1
Honours: 1 full cap for Scotland and 4 under-23 caps
    (before joining Ipswich)

Other clubs: Cowdenbeath, St Mirren, Tottenham Hotspur, Arsenal, Stoke City, Walsall and Crewe Alexandra.

---

performances attracted the attention of Tottenham Hotspur, where he became quite a star. He played for Scotland against Wales in 1965 and scored the first goal in Tottenham's 2-1 victory over Chelsea in the FA Cup final at Wembley in 1967. Then he moved across London to play for Arsenal (without all the controversy of Sol Campbell's move in 2001). He made 87 League appearances for the Gunners before his £55,000 move to Portman Road, where he was hailed as a saviour. Ipswich made a profit when they sold him to Stoke City for £80,000 in 1972, after he took Ipswich up on the agreement that he could move when he wanted. He made 99 starts for Stoke before finishing his career with Walsall and Crewe Alexandra. His departure left the opening for Mick Lambert to rise up from the youth team.

James Scowcroft
Forward, 1994 to 2001

Born: Bury St Edmunds, 15 November 1975
Signed: 1 July 1994 from youth scheme
Debut: *v.* Wolverhampton Wanderers (home),
　　lost 1-2, 7 October 1995

Ipswich career:
181 starts (47 subs), 54 goals
Premiership: 22(12), 4
Football League: 141(27), 43
Play-offs: 6(2), 1
FA Cup: 9(1)
Football League Cup: 24(4), 5
Anglo-Italian Cup: 1(1), 1
Honours: 5 England under-21 caps

Other club: Leicester City.

Ipswich supporters always seem to develop a special affinity with Suffolk-born players, but there was a time when James Scowcroft was being given a hard time by a section of the crowd in the North Stand. Happily, things changed for the better. His first hat-trick came in a 3-0 win at Crewe. In the 1999/2000 season he was voted Player of the Year, both by fans and by fellow players.

Scowcroft's first visit to Wembley was in an under-11 six-a-side competition before one of the non-League finals. Injury prevented him from taking his place in the memorable Division One play-off against Barnsley.

Many people attribute Marcus Stewart's fantastic goalscoring in Town's first season back in the Premiership to his understanding with Scowcroft, whose talent for hold-up play was certainly missed after his departure to Leicester in the summer of 2001. Maybe it was short of being telepathic, but it was considerably better than anyone else managed in the following season that saw relegation.

Scowcroft did my bank balance a world of good when Ipswich were drawn to meet Arsenal at Highbury in the Worthington Cup in November 2000. The Gunners were expected to field a number of reserves, so backing Ipswich at 5-1 looked particularly good value. I was kept on tenterhooks, though. Scowcroft netted an 89th-minute winner from a rebound after a shot from David Johnson had been blocked on the line by Matthew Upson.

One can understand Scowcroft, often on the bench at Ipswich, being keen to link up with his England under-21 coach Peter Taylor at Leicester. The snag was that Taylor did not stay long and Leicester had a season that turned out to be even more miserable than that at Ipswich.

Steve Sedgley

Defender or Midfield, 1994 to 1997

Steve Sedgley always gave the impression of being the most laid-back of footballers. He cost a club record £1 million pounds from Tottenham, but his overall contribution in the 1994/95 relegation season was disappointing. He did not see eye to eye with George Burley when the new manager took over from John Lyall. The outcome was that he was stripped of the captaincy and axed from the first team.

Sedgley patched up his differences the following season to help Ipswich recoup their fortunes in Division One. He was sold to Wolverhampton Wanderers in a deal that brought Mark Venus to Portman Road as well as a sizeable cheque.

Sedgley's career ended through injury. He left Molineux to coach Kingstonian. His father, Gordon, was an FA Amateur Cup winner with Wealdstone in 1966 and Enfield the following year. Steve was an unused Coventry substitute in the 1987 FA Cup final before moving to Tottenham for £750,000 in July 1989.

Born: Enfield, 26 May 1968
Signed: 15 June 1994 from Tottenham for
 £1 million
Debut: v. Norwich City (home), lost 1-2,
 19 September 1994

Ipswich career:
135 starts, 18 goals
Premiership: 26, 4
Football League: 89, 11
Play-offs: 2
FA Cup: 5
Football League Cup: 10
Anglo-Italian Cup: 3, 1
Honours: 11 England under-21 caps with Coventry
 and Tottenham between 1987 and 1990

Other clubs: Coventry City, Tottenham Hotspur,
 and Wolverhampton Wanderers.

Laurie Sivell
Goalkeeper, 1964 to 1984

Born: Lowestoft, 8 February 1951
Signed: 6 February 1969 as junior
Debut: *v.* Liverpool (away), lost 0-2,
    24 March 1970

Ipswich career:
175 starts
Football League: 141
FA Cup: 19
Football League Cup: 7
UEFA Cup: 7
Texaco Cup: 1

One of the shortest goalkeepers to play League football, he was also one of the bravest. Discovered by scout Reg Tyrrell in Lowestoft, Sivell served Ipswich Town over a period of fifteen years. In the 1974/75 season he played 40 League matches in a Town side that was only two points away from winning the Championship. Ipswich came third to Brian Clough's Derby County and Liverpool that campaign.

Sivell played in all nine FA Cup ties that season, including the dramatic four against Leeds United. The run ended with a heartbreaking semi-final replay defeat against West Ham at Stamford Bridge. Ipswich supporters will always remember the part played by referee Clive Thomas on that sorry night. All that time Paul Cooper, who had been signed from Birmingham City, was in the reserves.

Sivell never lost his confidence after picking the ball out of his net no less than seven times against Sheffield United at Bramall Lane in 1971. He will never forget, nor will anyone else present, the match at Villa Park on 6 March 1976. The score was 0-0 with only a minute left to play when Andy Gray challenged for a rebound after Sivell had blocked a shot from Chris Nicholl. Sivell dived ever so bravely at Gray's feet, saved a certain goal, but ended with his teeth kicked out and his face in such a state that there was an editorial decision not to publish the picture. One wonders how Gray would view an identical incident today in his role as a television pundit.

Sivell was also a useful club cricketer for Lowestoft. He played for Suffolk Club & Ground at Framlingham College and brought off a spectacular catch high above his head at extra cover. He strained his groin and was left with a problem. Ipswich Town had one more match, albeit a friendly, in which he was expected to play. The only solution was to break down in the warm-up – which is exactly what he did! Another strange injury he sustained resulted in a need for five stitches in a cut above his eye when playing squash. The club had a court under the Portman (now Cobbold) Stand.

Outside right, 1960 to 1965

Born: Crook Town, 27 May 1932
Died: January 2000
Signed: 14 July 1960 from Leicester City
Debut: v. Brighton & Hove Albion (home),
    won 4-0, 13 September 1960

Ipswich career:
163 starts, 26 goals
Football League: 144, 21
FA Cup: 8, 2
Football League Cup: 6, 2
European Cup: 4
FA Charity Shield: 1, 1

Other clubs: Burnley, Rotherham United, Blackburn
    Rovers and Leicester City.

In Roy Stephenson, Alf Ramsey found the ideal player to use in his tactical plan of feeding crack marksmen Ray Crawford and Ted Phillips from deep wide positions. With plenty of experience before arriving at Portman Road, Stephenson settled in well and enjoyed the area so much that he married and stayed for the rest of his life.

He was the son of a colliery electrician and was regarded as a useful footballer at Wolsingham Grammar School. As a sixteen-year-old he was given a trial by manager Cliff Britton at Burnley. Two years later he joined the ground staff at Turf Moor. He completed his apprenticeship as a mining engineer before starting football seriously at Burnley. He made more than 100 first-team appearances for the club and also played cricket for the town team in the Lancashire League, whose professionals at the time included the West Indian Bruce Pairaudeau and Peter Wight, who later played for Somerset.

Stephenson joined Rotherham United for £4,500 in 1956 to help the small Yorkshire club consolidate after winning promotion to the Second Division. As chance would have it, Ipswich were at Millmoor in Stephenson's second match for the club. The players arrived at the ground by coach, which parked on the tarmac between the Press box and the entrance to the players' dressing rooms. The Ipswich squad filed out, all except Stephenson who was lying along the floor of the coach between the seats. I

was still on the coach and asked him what was going on. Apparently some young lady, whom he must have known from his days as a Rotherham player, was waiting for him. He clearly preferred not to meet her, so wanted her to believe that he was not in the party. I was asked to keep watch until she had moved off. Once I had given the all-clear, he caught up with the other players.

Stephenson soon became a key member of the side. Not only could he create goals, but he had a powerful shot with either foot and picked up 9 goals in the Second Division championship run and then 7 in 41 games to help Ipswich take the title. He also scored against Tottenham in the Charity Shield, a match with FA Cup winners Tottenham played at Portman Road and won 5-1 by Bill Nicholson's side who had at last found a way to combat Ramsey's tactics.

After Rotherham, Stephenson had a spell at Blackburn under Johnny Carey. He was in the team that suffered the disappointment of an FA Cup semi-final defeat at the hands of Bolton Wanderers in 1958. His next move was to Leicester City, where he never really settled. He was looking for a move back to the North East, but finishing his career with Ipswich turned out to be a dream ending for a player who might otherwise have felt that he had underachieved.

He was soon invited to play cricket for my Saxmundham side and continued to play local club cricket and regular rounds of golf at Fynn Valley until his death.

Born: Chelmsford, 14 February 1965
Signed: 17 December 1982 from youth scheme
Debut: *v.* Coventry City (away), won 1-0,
    26 December 1985

Ipswich career:
555 starts (53 subs), 44 goals
Premiership: 94(2), 5
Football League: 370(40), 30
Play-offs: 4(1), 2
FA Cup: 28(3), 1
Football League Cup: 42(5), 5
Anglo-Italian Cup: 2
Full Members' Cup: 15(2), 1

Other club: Colchester United.

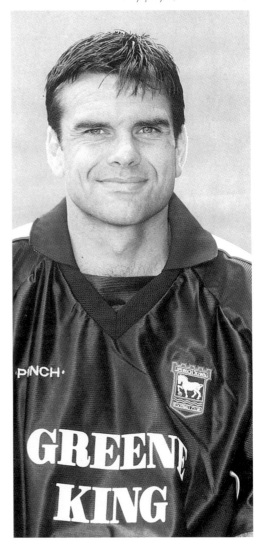

Mick Stockwell is one of those wholehearted players who won over the fans because of his total commitment to the cause. It was no surprise when he was voted Player of the Year when Ipswich returned to the Premiership under John Lyall and Mick McGiven in the 1992/93 season. He was the only ever-present player the following campaign, which underlined his dedication and loyalty.

Mick had a well-deserved testimonial in 1994 that included a golf day at Stoke-by-Nayland that was called off at short notice because the course was waterlogged. I recall joining up with Steve Whitton and fellow reporter Dave Allard in a pleasant public house in Dedham from which, by mid-evening, we were all grateful for a lift home.

Mick was versatile. He could play full-back or wide midfield, but I recall one occasion at Leicester when he looked as though he could do a splendid job up front. In fact he seemed to enjoy Filbert Street. In 1987/88 he pulled the ball back after a tremendous run for Neil Woods to score an equaliser. Two seasons later he fired home the winner against the run of play from Chris Kiwomya's low cross. But it was in October 1990 that, used as a makeshift striker, he scored twice in a 2-1 win at Leicester. He was set up by David Gregory on both occasions.

His parents were keen followers, both home and away. On one occasion outside the ground at Elm Park in Reading I was taken to task by Mr and Mrs Stockwell for giving Mick less than complimentary reports at a time when he was struggling to find his sharpest form after a spell out through injury. Needless to say I had nothing against Mick personally, but if he was not playing at his best what was I expected to write? He had trials at Leyton Orient before joining Ipswich.

On what he achieved in his short spell at Ipswich, he may not really be entitled to a place in *100 Greats* but his arrival certainly helped Ipswich retain First Division status in the 1983/84 season.

His playing career virtually came to a halt after he hurt his back in a car accident near Hintlesham late one night. Sunderland played in my Football Writers' Association-winning golf team at the RAC Club at Epsom in 1989 when Max Turner, winner of the Golf Illustrated Gold Vase, and journalist Dave Allard made up the quartet.

He bought a pub in Ipswich called The Halberd, but was not really cut out for that sort of business. He had a piece in an Arsenal programme suggesting that Gunners fans paid him a visit when they came to Ipswich. Little did he realise how popular he had become after scoring Arsenal's winner in the 1979 FA Cup final against Manchester United. The small pub was swamped with Arsenal fans, yet he had not thought of having extra bar staff or having a supply of sandwiches ready! Now he lives on the Maltese island of Gozo.

Born: Conisburgh, 1 July 1953
Signed: February 1984 for Arsenal
Debut: v. Southampton (home), lost 0-3,
   21 February 1984

Ipswich career:
44 starts (9 subs), 10 goals
Football League: 36(7), 8
FA Cup: 2(1), 1
Football League Cup: 6(1), 1
Honours: 1 England cap v. Austria in 1980,
   under-23 and under-21 caps

Other clubs: Wolverhampton Wanderers, Arsenal and Derry City.

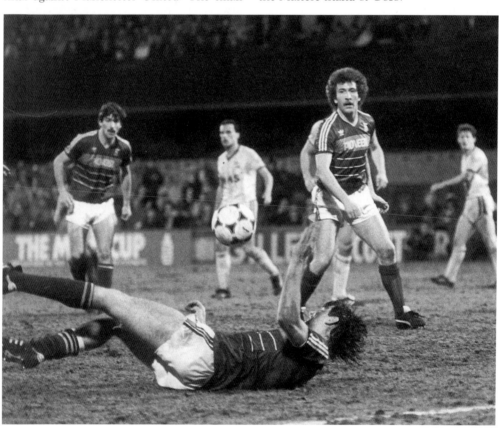

Brian Talbot
Midfield, 1970 and 1979

Born: Ipswich, 21 July 1953
Dsigned: 28 July 1970 from apprentice
Debut: *v.* Burnley (away), won 1-0,
    9 February 1974

Ipswich career:
227 starts, 31 goals
Football League: 177, 25
FA Cup: 23, 3
Football League Cup: 12, 1
UEFA Cup: 10, 2
European Cup Winners' Cup: 4
FA Charity Shield: 1
Honours: 6 England caps (5 at Ipswich),
    2 England B caps and one under-21 cap

Other clubs: Arsenal, Watford, Stoke City, West
    Bromwich, Fulham and Aldershot.

Brian made the most of his talent by sheer hard work in midfield. He ran, ran, and then ran some more to wear down the opposition. He gained such a great reputation that he became the first Ipswich-born player to win a full cap for England. Bobby Robson said: 'Sometimes I think he has got two hearts instead of one. I have never known a player get from box to box so quickly.'

There were many who underestimated the potential of the Tower Ramparts boy in those early days because of his lack of pace. He has never let me forget that I virtually wrote off his chances of being a regular first-team player! There were others who must have been thinking along similar lines because he was very close to joining Bournemouth for £40,000.

He made his debut at Burnley in 1974 after Colin Viljoen needed an Achilles tendon operation. He held his place consistently after that until the pinnacle of achievement, when he won FA Cup winners' medals in successive years.

He was in the Ipswich team of 1978 that beat Arsenal. The following season he joined the Gunners, who beat Manchester United 3-2 at Wembley. Talbot scored the first and Alan Sunderland grabbed the winner. He also appeared in the 1980 FA Cup final at Wembley, when Arsenal lost to West Ham.

Arsenal had good value from their £450,000 capture.

In the 1978 semi-final against West Bromwich at Highbury, Talbot opened the scoring after eight minutes. Unfortunately he clashed heads with Albion skipper John Wile. Talbot had to leave the field. Wile played on with blood seeping through his heavily bandaged forehead.

As manager of West Bromwich, Talbot once asked me to do a scouting report for him. Perhaps it wasn't that good because he never asked me again! He was the manager who lifted Rushden & Diamonds into the Football League.

Born: Buenos Aires, 10 March 1973
Signed: 9 August 1994 from Argentinos Juniors
Debut: *v.* Bolton Wanderers (Coca Cola Cup,
    home), lost 0-3, 21 September 1994

Ipswich career:
167 starts (3 subs), 6 goals
Football League: 134(3), 4
Play-offs: 4
FA Cup: 8
Football League Cup: 18, 2
Anglo-Italian Cup: 3
Honours: Argentina under-23

Other clubs: River Plate, Argentinos Juniors and
    Tottenham Hotspur.

Mauricio Taricco arrived in England as an Argentina under-23 international. He played for Argentinos Juniors, the same club as Diego Maradona and Fernando Redondo. His Town debut, as a frail-looking individual, was something of a disaster against Bolton Wanderers in a Coca Cola Cup defeat at Portman Road. He had to wait quite a while after that for his League debut because George Burley took a bit of convincing at first.

Mauricio stuck to his task, filled out well, and started to display the skills that Charlie Woods and John Lyall had spotted when they first saw him play in his own country. He arrived at the same time as Adrian Paz, the Uruguayan international, who had a bit of a raw deal at Ipswich because he was said to be 'an old fashioned English style centre forward'. In fact he turned out to be a skilful winger, but things were expected of him that he could not produce.

Taricco's father, Piero Nello, played for Juventus in the 1940s. There was football in his blood but he took time to learn the English language and become used to the physical side of the English game.

Once he and his wife, Evan, settled in to life in Suffolk his football career progressed by leaps and bounds. He was named in a sixty-strong Argentina pool for the Copa Americas while he was still at Ipswich, but his dreams of breaking into the Argentinian World Cup squad were dashed despite his bright Premiership form with Tottenham.

His most spectacular goal for Ipswich came in the Coca Cola Cup tie against Manchester United at Portman Road in October 1997. He wasted no time in sending the picture back to his family and friends in Argentina via the Internet. As it's a thirteen-hour flight back home, he does not make the trip too often. In that Coca Cola Cup run, Ipswich went on to beat Oxford United at the Manor Ground and then hold Chelsea after extra-time. Taricco and James Scowcroft were those who failed to find the net in the penalty shoot out.

Mauricio developed a hate-hate relationship with Sheffield United after Dane Whitehouse was sent off for a blow which apparently knocked Taricco to the ground. The arm was raised but there was precious little contact. This was why the fans at Bramall Lane were up in arms. It was ironic that Taricco conceded a penalty in a Cup tie at Bramall Lane in an incident with Marcelo. The Brazilian got the better of the Argentinian on that occasion – despite the fact that it never looked like a genuine spot kick.

Frans Thijssen
Midfield, 1979 to 1983

Born: Holland, 23 January 1952
Signed: 13 February 1979 from
    FC Twente Enschede
Debut: *v.* Derby County (away), won 1-0,
    28 February 1979

Ipswich career:
167 starts (3 subs), 16 goals
Football League: 123(2), 10
FA Cup: 15, 2
Football League Cup: 12(1)
UEFA Cup: 17, 4
Honours: Played for Holland 8 times while
    at Ipswich

Other clubs: FC Twente, Vancouver Whitecaps,
    Nottingham Forest and Fortuna Sittard.

Frans Thijssen was a real bargain at £220,000 from FC Twente Enschede. It was a sensational coup by Bobby Robson, who recognised the quality of this classy right-sided midfield player.

Arnold Muhren had already been at Portman Road for six months when Thijssen arrived. He also came from FC Twente and was delighted to renew an old partnership that looked sure to blossom from the outset.

The first of his 16 goals for the club was a winner against Norwich City at Carrow Road so he was a firm favourite with the Town fans from his very first season. He scored one goal in each leg of the 1981 UEFA Cup final against AZ 67 Alkmaar to help Ipswich to this prestigious European trophy. His efforts were recognised by the Football Writers' Association, who made him their player of the year.

The following season he was able to play in only a dozen First Division matches because of a stress fracture of the shin sustained at Liverpool. When he left Ipswich he had a brief spell with Vancouver Whitecaps before being tempted back into English football by Brian Clough who was then with Nottingham Forest.

He completed his playing career in his native Holland, spending a couple of seasons with Fortuna Sittard before coaching the youth team at Vitesse Arnhem. He also managed the famous Swedish club Malmo for a while. In 1991 Frans chose Ipswich Town for his testimonial match at Vitesse Arnhem. Bobby Robson, then coaching PSV Eindhoven, was guest of honour.

Neil Thompson

Defender, 1989 to 1995

Born: Beverley, 2 October 1963
Signed: 9 June 1989 from Scarborough for £100,000
Debut: v. Barnsley (home), won 3-1, 19 August 1989

Ipswich career:
233 starts (8 subs), 22 goals
Premiership: 72(1), 3
Football League: 122(6), 15
FA Cup: 17, 2
Football League Cup: 14(1), 1
Full Members' Cup: 8, 1

Other clubs: Nottingham Forest, Hull City (twice),
    Scarborough (twice), Barnsley, Oldham,
    York City and Boston United.

Neil Thompson and Mark Venus are two Ipswich Town footballers known for the power in their left boots. Both players have scored some marvellous goals with thunderbolts. Thompson joined Ipswich from Scarborough in 1989, but before that he had a spell as an apprentice with Nottingham Forest where he made little impression. Clearly he was a late developer.

Then he spent two seasons with Hull City before being released. His football at Scarborough was part-time and he also had jobs selling disposable nappies and then worked for a brewery. During this time he represented the England semi-professional side four times. He was with Scarborough when they won promotion to the Football League.

He became popular with Ipswich fans and it was something of a surprise when George Burley released him in 1995 to clear the decks for rebuilding. He still

had plenty to offer with Barnsley, whom he helped to promotion to the Premiership. Then it was back to Scarborough as player-manager before joining Boston United to give their defence a bit of stability on their run-in to pip Dagenham and Redbridge for a place in the Football League. He took over as manager in July 2002.

Claus Thomsen

Defender or midfield, 1994 to 1996

Born: Denmark, 31 May 1970
Signed: 15 June 1994 from Aarhus for £200,000
Debut: v. Manchester United (home), won 3-2,
    24 September 1994

Ipswich career:
92 starts (5 subs), 9 goals
Premiership: 31(2), 5
Football League: 46(2), 4
FA Cup: 5
Football League Cup: 8
Anglo-Italian Cup: 2(1)
Honours: Denmark international and former
    under-21 captain

Other clubs: Aarhus, Everton, AB Copenhagen
    and Wolfsburg.

Claus Thomsen was bought from Aarhus for £200,000 and sold to Everton for £900,000 with a sell-on clause, which meant that Ipswich had completed a shrewd piece of business. He made a winning debut against Manchester United in September 1994 and provided the cross from which Paul Mason scrambled home one of the goals. He ended that disastrous relegation season as Town's top marksman with 5 goals.

Thomsen enjoyed a successful Euro '96 with Denmark and had settled down well alongside Steve Sedgley in central defence when his problems began. He came back from playing for Denmark against Greece in October with a groin strain that developed into a hernia.

A former Danish under-21 captain, he was sold when fully fit to keep the books balanced. He is the sort of overseas player who contributed well both on the field and in the community.

Manager George Burley said: 'It was an offer we could not turn down. It's a big blow for us, but it's a great move for Claus. Everton have given him a long contract which really makes him for life.' It did not, in fact, work out too well for Claus on Merseyside and he returned to the Continent to play first in Denmark and then for Wolfsburg in the Bundesliga.

Colin Viljoen ————————————————————————

Inside forward, 1967 to 1978

Colin Viljoen arrived from South Africa on the recommendation of Johannesburg Rovers' coach Gordon Edleston, a friend of Bill McGarry. A work permit was an early problem, so Viljoen's early football was played when registered as John Cobbold's gardener at Glemham Hall. It is doubtful if Viljoen could tell a gladioli bulb from an onion, but that hardly mattered.

It became obvious that he was a talented player, although there was a scare for Town at the start of 1967/68 season when there was a rumour that he might not return from his holiday in South Africa. McGarry flew out to resolve the matter by offering Viljoen terms as a full-time professional now that he had completed his two-year residential qualification.

He scored a hat-trick on his debut at home to Portsmouth and made such an impression that, once he had secured English citizenship, he was picked for England by Don Revie against Northern Ireland and Wales in 1975. He became a midfield player with an eye for goal. He was known as 'Ace' by his colleagues in the dressing room and seemed to have his own views when it came to tactics and how to approach games.

When he became manager, McGarry wanted to learn how to play squash. He

Born: Johannesburg, 20 June 1948
Signed: 14 August 1967 as amateur
Debut: *v.* Portsmouth (home), won 4-2,
　　25 March 1967

Ipswich career:
367 starts (2 subs), 45 goals
Football League: 303(2), 45
FA Cup: 28(1), 6
Football League Cup: 20, 2
UEFA Cup: 11(2), 1
Texaco Cup: 5
Honours: 2 full caps for England in 1975 versus
　　Northern Ireland and Wales

Other clubs: Manchester City and Chelsea.

———————————————————————

asked me to take him to the courts at the Ipswich Airport (where the roof leaked and there were often puddles in the corner after rain). I taught McGarry the basics. Then he practised on the apprentices, making the playing of squash a compulsory part of training! Viljoen was one of those who felt that squash was likely to do very little for his football. Coach Sammy Chung was a better squash player than McGarry, but it wasn't a good decision to beat the boss.

It was easy to feel a degree of sympathy for

Colin Viljoen (right) leaps to head the ball in a match at Portman Road in the days of the old Portman Road stand. The stand was sold to Foxhall Stadium, where it blew down in gales.

Viljoen in 1978. He had been out with injury for a long while as Ipswich overcame hurdle after hurdle to the FA Cup final without him. Bobby Robson was considering recalling 'Ace' for the big day at Wembley to the exclusion, it seemed, of local lad Roger Osborne.

Robson visualised a midfield feast of football with Viljoen pitting his wits against Arsenal's Liam Brady. In the last League match before the final, Ipswich were away at Aston Villa. Viljoen was brought into the side but the decision clearly did not go down at all well with the other players who felt that Osborne had played a big part in get-

ting them to Wembley and should not be denied his chance on the big day.

Ipswich were hammered 6-1 at Villa Park. Robson was understandably upset, but he got the message. Osborne played at Wembley to become the unlikely hero. A dejected and angry Viljoen dropped out of the Town squad preparing for Wembley and never played for the club again. It was a sorry end to a sparkling few years at Portman Road. He joined Manchester City and then moved to Chelsea. He ran a public house called Nine Stiles near New Denham for a while before returning to live in South Africa.

Born: Glasgow, 4 August 1957
Signed: 13 August 1975 as junior
Debut: *v.* Leeds United (FA Cup sixth round third
    replay at Leicester), won 3-2, 27 March 1975

Ipswich career:
670 starts (8 subs), 190 goals
Premiership: 100(1), 13
Football League: 433(5), 122
FA Cup: 55(1), 12
Football League Cup: 42(1), 25
UEFA Cup: 19, 16
European Cup Winners' Cup: 6
Anglo-Italian Cup: 2
FA Charity Shield: 1
Full Members' Cup: 12, 2
Honours: 29 full caps for Scotland, 8 under-21 caps
    and youth caps. PFA Player of Year and
    European Young Footballer of the Year in 1981.

Other clubs: Liverpool and Middlesbrough.

———————————————————————

John Wark, strange as it may seem, won the Ipswich Player of the Year award on three occasions all towards the end of his illustrious career. The year he was voted PFA Player of the Year in 1981, the Ipswich fans voted for goalkeeper Paul Cooper – perhaps as a consolation because he was the only regular at the time without international caps. Frans Thijssen was the FWA Player of the Year that season, so it was something of a clean sweep at Portman Road.

A Scotsman from Glasgow, Wark arrived in Ipswich as a youth player and made his debut as a seventeen-year-old. At first he was terribly homesick, but he was thrown in at the deep end in an FA Cup sixth round third replay with Leeds United, one of the most powerful sides in the land, on a neutral ground at Leicester City. Wark played alongside Allan Hunter, whose calming influence helped the young Scot through the ordeal. He could have joined Manchester City, but was right to think that his prospects would be better under Bobby Robson.

At the height of his career, Wark was playing in midfield where he developed the knack of making late runs into the opposition penalty area and grabbing crucial goals. This was especially valuable in Europe, where he scored 14 UEFA Cup goals in 12 matches to share the record set by Jose Altafini of AC Milan and Lothar Emmerich of Borussia Dortmund. Three of Wark's goals came from the penalty spot against Aris Salonika. Altafini's goals were scored in 1962/63 when Milan, the eventual European Cup winners, beat Ipswich in the second round. In his first spell at Portman Road, Wark won an FA Cup Winners' medal in 1978 and an UEFA Cup Winners' medal in 1981. Ipswich were also runners-up to Aston Villa and Liverpool in successive seasons.

Wark moved away to Liverpool for £450,000 in 1984. He had asked for a transfer. As he knew Graeme Souness, Kenny Dalglish and Alan Hansen from playing for Scotland, he jumped at the chance when Joe Fagan showed an interest. At Anfield he picked up a League Championship medal and added three more Scottish caps to bring his overall total to 29. He had also previously won youth caps and 8 under-21 caps. He missed a full season at Anfield with a broken ankle, an injury that was followed by damage to his Achilles tendon. He was in plaster twice during his years on Merseyside.

In January 1988, John Duncan brought Wark back to Portman Road where he was player of the year, but in the summer of 1990 he accepted a two-year deal at Middlesbrough, who were prepared to pay him more at the time than Ipswich, who received a nominal £50,000 fee.

Manager Colin Todd left Boro in June 1991. New boss Lennie Lawrence released him with a year of his contract still to run because he wanted his players to live in the North East. Boro had used him in midfield while, at that stage of his career, a defensive role was more suitable as there was far less running.

He had chances to join Coventry City and Colchester United (who were then in the Conference), but decided to bide his time and train with Ipswich although John Lyall was not too keen at first to offer him a deal. Ipswich then had an injury crisis in defence. Wark was thrown into the side in an away game at Grimsby, played extremely well, and held his place in what turned out to be a Second Division Championship-winning side.

Even though he was on a weekly contract, he became an automatic choice. The big question was whether he would still be able to handle life in the Premiership. As everyone now knows, his ability to read the game so well made up for any lack of pace. He was never daunted about having to mark the best strikers in the game. He took it all in his stride.

After he hung up his boots he did a bit of scouting for George Burley before being appointed as chief scout at Portsmouth, a job that lasted until massive changes at Fratton Park took place after the departure of manager Alan Ball. Now he works at Portman Road, helping with corporate entertaining.

'Warky' was also a bit of a film star in *Escape to Victory* with Michael Caine, Sylvester Stallone and several other footballers. Paul Mariner was best man at his wedding and they have maintained a close friendship ever since.

Two Ipswich legends find themselves in opposition. John Wark (right) finds himself competing with Jason Dozzell, then of Tottenham Hotspur, in a match at Portman Road.

Born: Burston, Norfolk, 4 May 1950
Signed: 5 May 1969 from Diss Town
Debut: *v.* Manchester City (away), lost 0-1,
    28 February 1970

Ipswich career:
322 starts (13 as sub), 104 goals
Football League: 249(12), 75 goals
FA Cup: 21, 2
Football League Cup: 20, 9
UEFA Cup: 20, 13
European Cup Winners' Cup: 3 (1)
Texaco Cup: 8, 5
FA Charity Shield: 1
Honours: 1 full England cap and 7 under-23 caps.

Other clubs: Derby County, Sparta Rotterdam,
    Grimsby Town, Vancouver Whitecaps,
    Southend United, Peterborough United,
    Colchester United and Diss Town (player-manager).

Trevor Whymark was one of the excellent home-produced players inherited by Bobby Robson and discovered by Town scout Reg Tyrrell. One of the best headers of the ball the club has ever had on the books, he won an England cap as a substitute against Luxembourg in 1978. He deserved more.

A Norfolk lad, Trevor enjoyed a glory night on 24 October 1973 when he put all four goals into the Lazio net in the UEFA Cup second round first leg tie at Portman Road. When he went to Italy for the second leg, he was presented with a plaque to mark his feat. This was arranged by none other than AC Roma, Lazio's biggest rivals who share the Olympic Stadium. This caused terrific ill feeling and certainly contributed to the troubles that followed in the second leg. He developed a taste for four-goal hauls, doing the same to West Bromwich in a First Division match in November 1976. It's not that Albion were a bad side, they finished seventh in the top flight that season. Four more came against Swedish minnows Landskrona Bois in the UEFA Cup in September 1977. Sadly, Trevor was carried off at Norwich on Boxing Day that season with strained knee ligaments. It was an injury that was to cost him his place in the FA Cup final at Wembley against Arsenal.

His name appeared in the official programme and VIP guest Mrs Maggie Thatcher, unaware of any change, is said to have voiced the opinion that Whymark had played well. Whymark took success and disappointment in his stride. In 1970 he overcame a gashed heel that needed ten stitches and needed a

What on earth is Bobby Robson hunting for in Trevor Whymark's hair? The caption at the time suggested that he was seeking out grey hairs at a players' reunion in 1990. The picture was taken on the balcony of the Ipswich Town Hall.

long, long time to heal. He was a credit to his profession. Now he coaches at the Ipswich Town Academy. If he can teach any of the lads to head a ball like he did in his prime, then he will have done the club a tremendous service.

Born: Cwmpare, South Wales, 5 January 1962
Signed: 1 July 1992 from Derby County for
    £650,000
Debut: *v.* Aston Villa (home), drawn 1-1,
    15 August 1992

Ipswich career:
263 appearances (1 sub), 2 goals
Premiership: 109, 1
Football League: 108, 1
Play-offs: 2
FA Cup: 18
Football League Cup: 24(1)
Anglo-Italian Cup: 2
Honours: 13 Welsh international caps (2 with
    Ipswich Town), 2 under-21 and youth caps

Other clubs: Bristol Rovers, Derby County and
    Colchester United.

Geraint Williams, who likes to be known as 'George', was one of the players John Lyall signed to help the club consolidate in the Premiership in 1992. A Welsh international midfield player, guaranteed to work tremendously hard, he was just the type of player needed at the time. Williams became first team captain and led by example. He was an excellent club ambassador.

The day after he was signed from Derby County, I was at the Hurlingham Club in London covering the national croquet championships. The lady running the public relations company promoting the croquet came from Derby. She heard that I was based in Ipswich. Halfway through a lobster salad washed down by Pimms she said that she had dinner with Derby County chairman Lionel Pickering the previous evening. She said: 'Lionel was in tremendous form. He said he had just sold a footballer to Ipswich for £650,000 and had thrown the Zimmer frame in free.' Perhaps I should not have used the story at the time of Lyall's resignation because Williams was still a key player at Portman Road. Now that he has hung up his boots and is coaching at Colchester he might see the funny side of it all.

He gave Ipswich excellent service but used to say: 'I am only named as man of the match when the team has played badly'. This was probably true because he could never be faulted for lack of endeavour. He was one of the many youngsters from South Wales who joined Bristol Rovers during the 1970s and was taken on as an apprentice in 1978. Although his goals were few and far between, he recalls scoring from the penalty spot for the Bristol Rovers youth team in a cup tie at Portman Road.

He moved to Derby County in March 1985 and helped the Rams rise from the Third Division to the First Division in successive seasons under manager Arthur Cox. He played for Wales against West Germany in the first international to be played at Cardiff Arms Park in front of 30,000 where he recalls that the atmosphere was fantastic.

He was out of contract at Derby in 1992 when he joined Ipswich. This was before the Bosman Ruling. He explained his reasons for the move when he said: 'The club had been restructured and were beginning to bring in players costing £1 million. I felt some of the long-serving players like myself were being taken for granted a little bit. The new arrivals were given better deals. I spoke to John Lyall who told me I was the type of player Ipswich needed. He made me feel wanted and valued. It turned out to be a good move for me.'

Kevin Wilson

Forward, 1985 to 1987

Born: Banbury, 18 April 1961
Signed: 5 January 1985 from Derby County
    for £150,000
Debut: v. Aston Villa (away), lost 1-2,
    2 February 1984

Ipswich career:
121 starts (4 subs), 49 goals
Football League: 94(4), 34
Play-offs: 2
FA Cup: 10, 3
Football League Cup: 10, 8
Full Members Cup: 5, 4
Honours: 42 caps for Northern Ireland

Other clubs: Chelsea, Notts County, Bradford
    City, Walsall and Northampton Town.

Kevin Wilson was recruited from Derby County for a bargain £150,000. Rams' manager, Arthur Cox, thought at first that Bobby Ferguson wanted Bobby Davison who went to Leeds. He soon regretted selling Wilson so cheaply and tried to get him back.

Wilson was a bargain buy at a time when funds were short because of the ill-advised decision to develop the Pioneer Stand without first arranging the funding. Wilson started his career with Northern Ireland only after Ferguson had informed the Irish FA that the lad had an Irish mother, a fact discovered by skipper Ian Atkins and passed on.

Nicknamed 'Jocky', for a reason obvious to those who follow darts, Wilson was ever-present in the 1986/87 season when an injury-ravaged

Ipswich failed in the play-offs against Charlton. That spelt the end of Ferguson's reign as manager. Wilson, out of contract, had no-one at Portman Road with whom he was prepared to negotiate a new deal. He moved to Chelsea for £300,000, but would have been happy to stay but for the treatment handed out to the manager who signed him. He found it tough at first at Stamford Bridge behind Kerry Dixon and Gordon Durie in the pecking order. Then he broke though.

He scored hat-tricks for Ipswich against Stoke City, Crystal Palace, Blackburn and Darlington (in the Milk Cup).

Winger 1969 to 1980

Clive Woods will always be remembered for his marvellous display against Arsenal in the FA Cup at Wembley in 1978. The stage seemed to be set just for him. He ran rings round the Gunners.

Another highlight in his career was the curling left-foot shot that gave Ipswich Town victory over Leeds United in an FA Cup third replay at Leicester in March 1975.

Skilful on the ball and entertaining to watch, he should never have been over-looked by England. He was once picked for a squad but never won a cap. Perhaps it was because Ipswich were still regarded as unfashionable by the establishment, despite what they had already achieved.

Clive should never be confused with Charlie Woods, who was a speed merchant

Born: Norwich, 18 December 1947
Signed: 19 June 1969 from Norwich Gothic
Debut: *v.* Newcastle United (home), won 2-0,
    6 September 1969

Ipswich career:
278 starts (60 subs), 31 goals
Football League: 217(50), 24
FA Cup: 24(4), 2
Football League Cup: 13(3), 2
UEFA Cup: 17(1), 1
European Cup Winners Cup: 5
FA Charity Shield: 1
Texaco Cup: 1(2), 2

Other club: Norwich City.

Clive Woods crosses, beating the challenge of Manchester City defender Ray Ranson at Portman Road in March 1979.

on the right wing on the same day that Clive made his debut as a substitute against Newcastle.

Charlie Woods stayed in football as a coach and scout without putting his head on the block as a manager. Joe Royle once said: 'If there was an atomic explosion I'd choose to stand beside Charlie Woods. He's a great survivor.'

Clive was a Norfolk boy who ended his League career with Norwich City before continuing to play for Newton Flotman just for the fun of it. The chance to join FC Twente was turned down because the money on offer was not enough to make it worthwhile uprooting his family. Like most wingers there were times when he may have been regarded as a luxury, but that tends to be the way with football managers.

Clive was a cricketer. I co-opted him into the British Press cricket team to play the Whitbread Taverners in an all-day charity match at Southill Park in Bedfordshire in the late 1970s. The Taverners included Allan Border (who scored a century) and were captained by Brian Close. The Press side, even with the Ipswich lads and Antiguan Hercules Grant (who had been playing for Suffolk), were outgunned.

Born: Ipswich, 5 November 1977
Signed: 2 January 1995 from being trainee
Debut: *v.* Coventry City (home), won 2-0,
     6 May 1995

Ipswich career:
291 starts
Premiership: 39
Football League: 201
Play-offs: 9
FA Cup: 13
Football League Cup: 27
Anglo-Italian Cup: 2
Honours: 2 full England caps, 15 under-21 caps
     and youth caps.

Other club: Arsenal and Everton.

The year Richard Wright signed professional forms for his home-town club he found the main obstacle in his way was Canadian international Craig Forrest, who had been voted player of the season. Town manager George Burley recognised the talent the youngster possessed and wasted no time in giving him a taste of football at the top level. Wright soon became a member of the England under-21 squad, but gives great credit to his goalkeeping coach Malcolm Webster for his rapid progress.

Wright really hit the headlines in the national press in January 1996 when he turned in a superb display in an FA Cup replay at Blackburn. He had been a professional for just over a year and faced a star-studded Rovers attack that included Alan Shearer. To add spice to the night, it was Shearer who had said the previous season that 'there are no easy games in the Premiership except Ipswich'. No one gave Ipswich much of a chance, but teenager Wright brought off half a dozen saves out of the top drawer. Paul Mason scored an extra-time winner for Ipswich, but it was Wright whose name was on the lips of all those in the Press box.

By now Wright was just about established. He became an automatic choice at Portman Road with Forrest moving on to West Ham. Wright broke into the full England squad but his debut in Malta was something of a nightmare. He conceded two penalties, saving one of them. A few days previously he had conceded another penalty in the showpiece Division One play-off against Barnsley at Wembley.

He was back to his consistent best on Town's return to the Premiership, when they finished in fifth place and qualified for the UEFA Cup. He thought long and hard about signing an extended contract at Portman Road and eventually did so when it was agreed that

Ipswich would not stand in his way if one of the 'big' clubs came in with a specified offer.

In the summer of 2001, Wright moved to Arsenal for £5 million. It looked as though he had every chance of deposing the veteran David Seaman, but it did not work out that way in his first season at Highbury. Wright, short of regular Premiership football, lost his place in Sven Goran Eriksson's England World Cup squad in Japan and South Korea. England opted for Seaman, Nigel Martyn of Leeds and David James of West Ham.

Another disappointment for Wright was to be left out of the FA Cup final against Chelsea in the Millennium Stadium in Cardiff. Wright had played in the earlier rounds.

Many Ipswich fans believe that Ipswich would never have been relegated in May 2002 if Wright had stayed for another season at Portman Road. It's hypothetical, but I tend to share that opinion and believe that good form for Ipswich would have kept him in the England squad. He joined Everton for £3 million in the summer of 2002.

Frank Yallop

Defender, 1982 to 1996

Born: Watford, 4 April 1964
Signed: 1 January 1982 from apprentice
Debut: *v.* Everton (away), lost 0-1, 17 March 1983

Ipswich career:
344 starts (36 subs), 8 goals
Premiership: 48(6), 3
Football League: 235(21), 4
Play-offs: 2
FA Cup: 15(3)
Football League Cup: 23(2), 1
Anglo-Italian Cup: 1(2)
Full Members' Cup: 20(2)
Honours: Canadian full international,
    5 England youth international caps.

Other clubs: Blackpool (loan), Tampa Bay Mutiny
    and San Jose Earthquakes (coach).

United the same week.

Always popular with the fans, he was player of the year at Portman Road in 1987/88. When he and his wife Karen left for the United States in 1996, he said: 'Even though I may not be the greatest player ever, I really miss the relationship with the fans. It has been fantastic.' He is playing a leading role in helping to establish Major League Soccer in the States. He started as a player with Tampa Bay Mutiny. In 2001 he was voted top coach in the land after transforming the fortunes of San Jose Earthquakes.

Although he won 5 caps for England youths, he was also eligible to play for Canada and took that option. An enormous amount of red tape needed to be cut to make it possible. When living in Ipswich he had a Great Dane called Harley. When exercising the dog he would often run into former manager Bobby Ferguson with his Alsatian and talk over old times. Yallop enjoys golf. If he had time to play regularly his handicap would drop dramatically.

Frank Yallop was nineteen years old when he made his debut against Everton at Goodison Park and found himself up against Andy Gray and Graeme Sharp. He was standing-in for George Burley, but began to play regularly after Burley moved to Sunderland. Yallop, by no means a regular marksman, hit a purple patch in 1992/93 season. He cracked in a great goal in a 2-0 win over Tottenham at White Hart Lane. Then he scored the decider at home to Manchester

Romeo Zondervan

Utility player, 1984 to 1992

Born: Surinam, 4 March 1959
Signed: 21 March 1984 from West Bromwich
    Albion for £70,000
Debut: *v.* Watford (home), drawn 0-0,
    24 March 1984

Ipswich career;
319 starts (6 subs), 20 goals
Football League 270(4), 13
Play-offs: 2
FA Cup: 11(2), 2
Football League Cup: 24, 3
Full Members' Cup: 12, 2
Honours: 6 full caps for Holland.

Other clubs: Postalia, Den Haag, FC Twente, West
    Bromwich Albion and NAC Breda.

After the glorious heady days of Arnold Muhren and Frans Thijssen at Portman Road, Romeo Zondervan became the third Dutch international player to join the Ipswich staff. Bobby Ferguson had originally spotted him playing for FC Twente, but his first club in England was West Bromwich Albion, who he had joined for £225,000 in 1982 following his friend Martin Jol to The Hawthorns.

A player of quality, Zondervan always seemed to have the ability to play within himself. Ferguson signed him to replace John Wark who had gone to Liverpool for £450,000 (most of the money needed to pay for the Pioneer Stand). Romeo never seemed rushed and was voted Ipswich player of the year in 1987. In his younger days he was Holland's 'most promising player' in 1981.

Ipswich secured a marvellous win over Manchester United at Old Trafford in May 1984 that went a long way to saving the club from relegation. Manager Bobby Ferguson, studying the team sheet, mistakenly went into the wrong dressing room. He saw a shirtless Remi Moses from the back, assumed it was Romeo, and started to gave his team talk to an astonished Manchester United squad. Ron Atkinson, the United manager, stopped him before he had gone too far. Ferguson told his own players what has happened, eased the tension with laughter, and hardly needed to talk tactics after that.

Romeo played for NAC Breda for a while before acting as a players' agent, sending hopefuls, such as Gus Uhlenbeek, to English clubs for trials. Now Romeo is an Ipswich Town part-time European scout. He is also a fully qualified pilot.

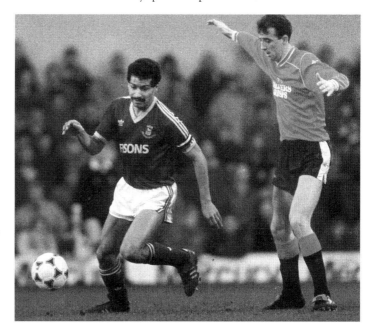

Romeo Zondervan (left) was a shrewd signing by Ipswich manager Bobby Ferguson, at a time when funds were short. He was club captain during a difficult period in the club's history.

No Ipswich Town book would be complete without a reminder of that great day at Wembley in 1978 when Roger Osborne's goal beat Arsenal in the FA Cup final. The joy at winning is obvious in this picture. From left to right, back row: Roger Osborne, Mick Mills, Brian Talbot, Clive Woods, Tommy Eggleston (physiotherapist), Mick Lambert, Russell Osman, Paul Cooper. Front row: Paul Mariner, John Wark, George Burley, David Geddis.